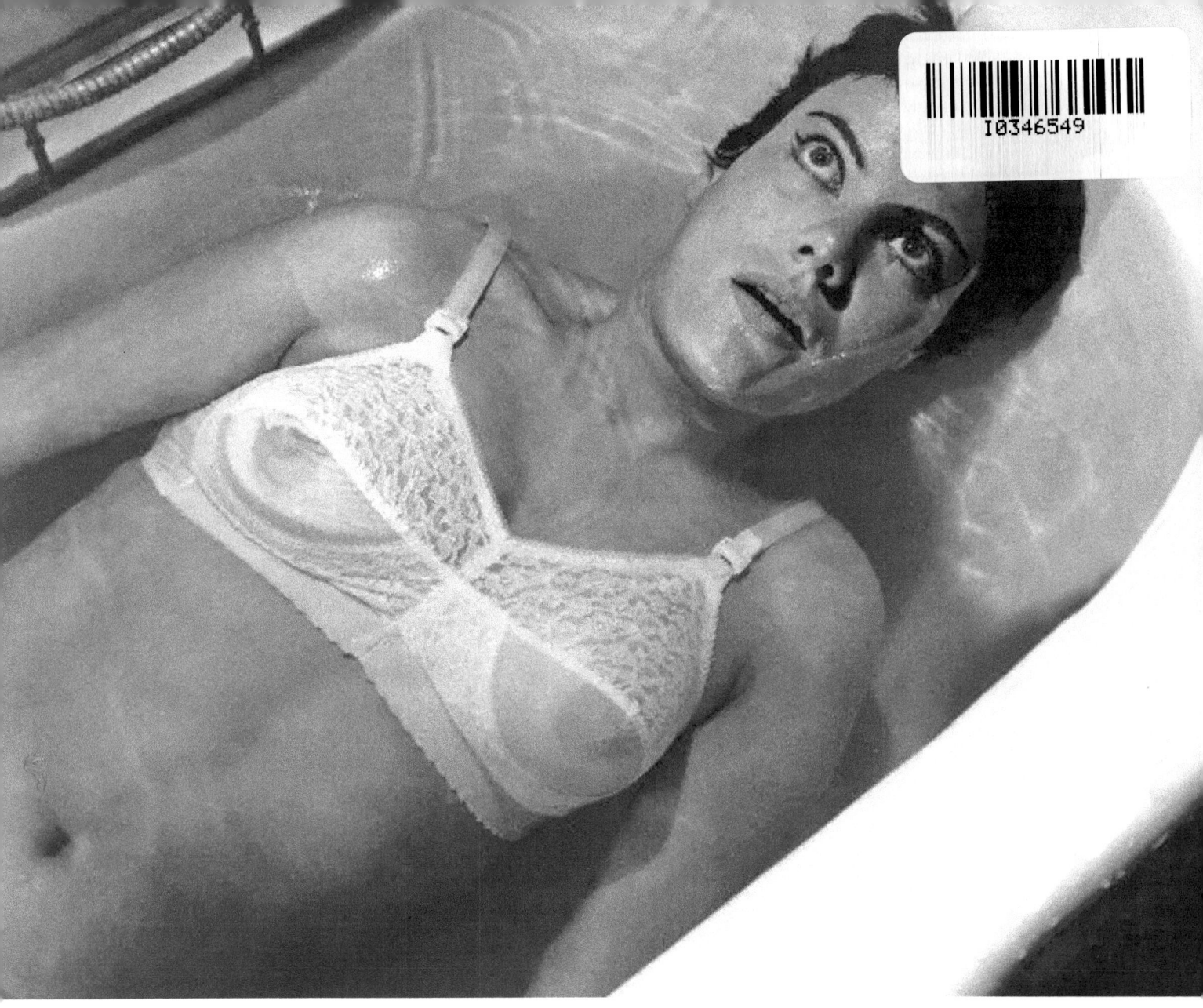

ORGY PLUS MASSACRE

SEXY, SCARY & SENSATIONAL CINEMA
1950-1979

VOLUME 4 (1963-1964)

CREDITS

ORGY + MASSACRE V.4
ISBN 978-1-917285-63-6
Edited by G.H. Janus
Text and images copyright © Black Gas Entertainment 2025
https://black-gas.org
Published by Black Gas Books 2025
In association with The Nocturne Group
All world rights reserved
Design template copyright © Broken Fang Cryptography
Published under licence from Fabbrica Sodoma Productions

CONTENTS

FOREWORD	005
HORROR	007
MAYHEM	027
MYTH	055
SCI-FI	071
SEX	107
INDEX	133

FOREWORD

After working with the Nocturne Group on two anthologies of material selected from their ongoing series of books on early cinema,[1] I was delighted when they offered me the chance to edit a new set of film books using photographs and previously unpublished texts from their post-1949 archive. This mass of material was originally to be developed for inclusion in their original series, but was set aside when it became clear that to produce books equally in-depth for the years 1950 onwards would take decades. Instead, I now have the opportunity to include a selection of these basic but still informative texts to enhance this collection of rare production stills.

As such, the ORGY PLUS MASSACRE series will present a visually-led sampling of sexy, scary and sensational cinema from the years 1950 to 1979, three of the most consequential decades in film history. It was during these years that global cinema came of age, not only in the technological sense but especially by way of pushing back the old restrictions of censorship, so much so that by the end of the 1960s, explicit sex and graphic violence had both become accepted in the mainstream. This new liberalism peaked in the mid-70s, when pretty much anything could be legally seen on commercially available film in one form in another, from picture houses to backstreet projection booths. Of course, this provoked an inevitable backlash in the 1980s, but ORGY PLUS MASSACRE will focus purely on these years when film-makers were free to express their most expansive, excessive and extreme visions on celluloid.

Volume ? includes more than 150 rare and unusual photographs, with accompanying texts, from the years 19?? to 19??. The book is divided into five sections: Horror, Mayhem (delinquency, crime, murder, atrocity), Myth (fantasies of the near and distant past), Science Fiction, and last but not least, Sex (nudity, sexploitation, pornography[2]). When a film falls into more than one category, as many do, the most dominant theme was chosen.

I now look forward to working on the next volumes of this series, with each one revealing how cinema grew sexier, scarier and more sensational with every passing year.

–G.H. Janus

1. The series from the Nocturne Group is entitled SHADOWS IN A PHANTOM EYE, and documents the years 1872 to 1949. I have edited two anthologies of material taken from the series, SATANIC SHADOWS and BEASTS AND BEAUTIES. These represent just a fraction of the content that the series, which runs to 15 volumes and well over 3,000 pages, has to offer.

2. Yes, even in the 1950s and 1960s loops of pornographic film were available, screened in the most clandestine venues or sold under counters, a situation which continued until Denmark led the legalization of such material from 1968 onwards.

KAIDAN ONI-BI NO NUMA
("Ghost Story Of The Demon-Fire Swamp")
Production: Japan, 1963
Director: Bin Kato
Category: Horror

HORROR

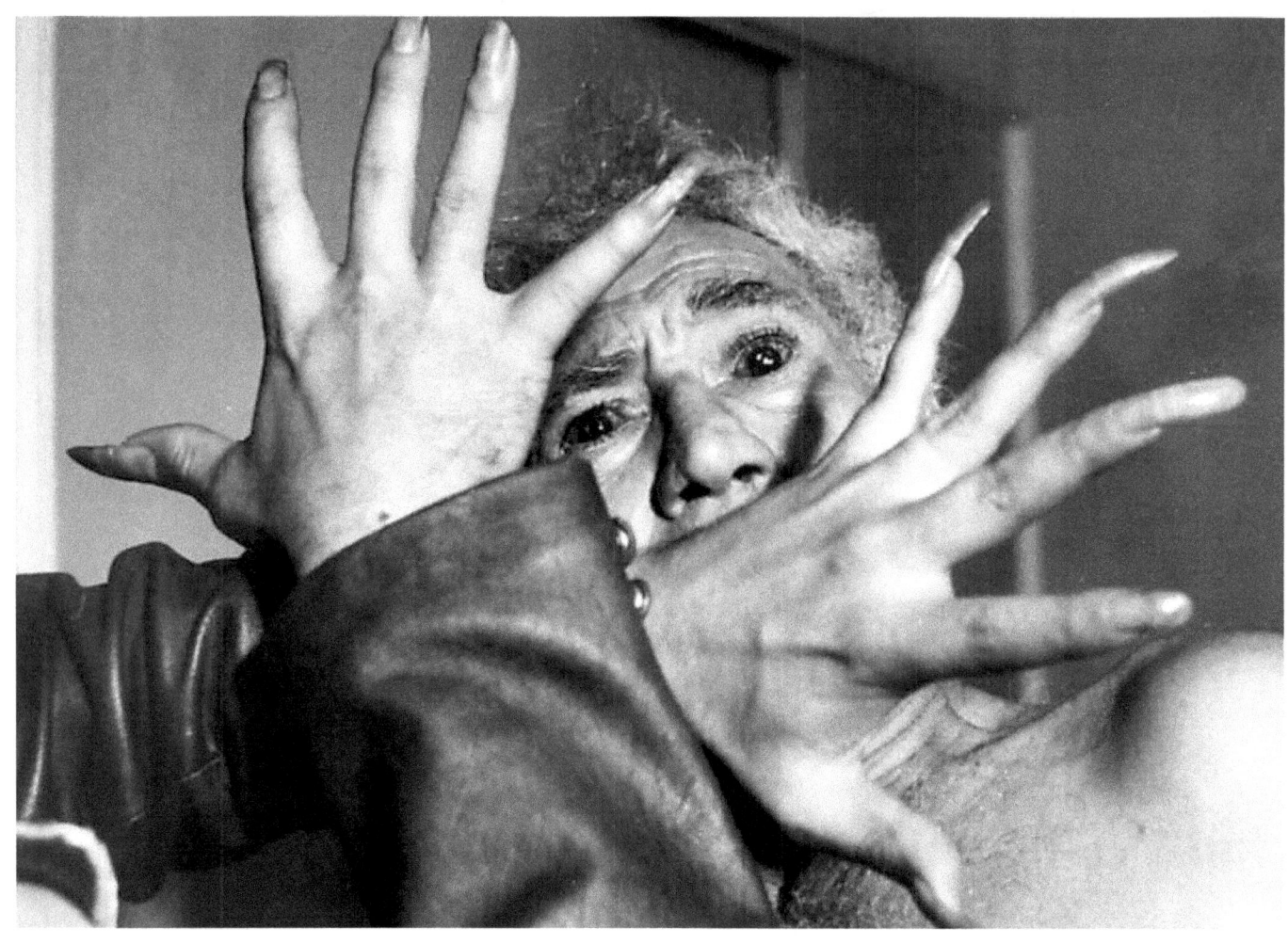

À MEIA-NOITE LEVAREI SUA ALMA
("At Midnight I'll Take Your Soul")
Production: Brazil, 1963-64
Director: José Mojica Marins
Category: Horror

Not only the first proper horror film ever made in Brazil, **À Meia-Noite Levarei Sua Alma** is also the first dark masterpiece by José Mojica Marins. Marins himself plays the role of village undertaker Zé do Caixão ("Coffin Joe"), a bearded graveyard dandy in black top hat and cape. Zé, who has bizarre philosophies to match his appearance, cruelly holds sway over the superstitious locals, whom he holds in absolute contempt; in several scenes, he espouses a nihilistic credo which is part anti-religion, part Nietzschean intellectual supremacy. But above all, Zé – who is searching for a woman to bear him a son in order to continue his "superior" bloodline – is a sadist capable of stupendous acts of violence (signalled by his eyes – filmed in close-up – becoming bloodshot). These include severing a man's fingers with a broken bottle, horse-whipping a man in a bar-fight, beating a woman to bloody pulp before raping her, and destroying a doctor's eyes with his long fingernails before setting the wretch on fire. He also murders his wife – who is barren and therefore of no use to him – by tarantula bite, and brutally smashes another man's skull with a poker before drowning him. Zé's atheism is finally tested after his rape victim curses him – "at midnight I'll take your soul!" – before hanging herself, and the local witch hounds him with prophesies of infernal damnation. In a drunken rage, the undertaker smashes up his own candlelit cemetery whilst screaming curses at the dead; later, during a violent thunderstorm, he is tormented by the voices of his victims and accusers, and shouts a challenge to Satan himself to appear and prove his existence. This leads to the film's climactic sequence, a *tour-de-force* in which Zé, walking alone through the forest during the Night of the Dead, becomes more and more agitated and apprehensive; finally he sees the bloody ghost of the man he drowned, followed by the procession of the dead (shot in negative), who are carrying his own body in a burial casket. Returning to the morgue, Zé is driven to break open the coffins of his victims – the scene closes with his soul-rending scream as he beholds the rotting corpses, crawling with maggots and spiders. When the villagers find him, he is sprawled upside-down, his face contorted and disfigured, eyes bulging hideously and sightlessly; the clock strikes midnight. Running for around 80 minutes, **À Meia-Noite Levarei Sua Alma** is a weird oneiric framing of sadism, sexual mania, psychosis, blasphemy and metaphysical rage, visually adorned with all the accoutrements of voodoo, black magic and the grave. Its disturbing ambience is enhanced by a cacophonous soundtrack of screams, evil laughter, electronic noise, storms, discordant music, and massive reverb on the actor' voices. It was a huge – and unexpected – hit in Brazil, the start of a long career in screen terror for Marins.

THE BIRDS
Production: USA, 1963
Director: Alfred Hitchcock
Category: Horror

BLACK ZOO
Production: USA, 1963
Director: Robert Gordon
Category: Horror

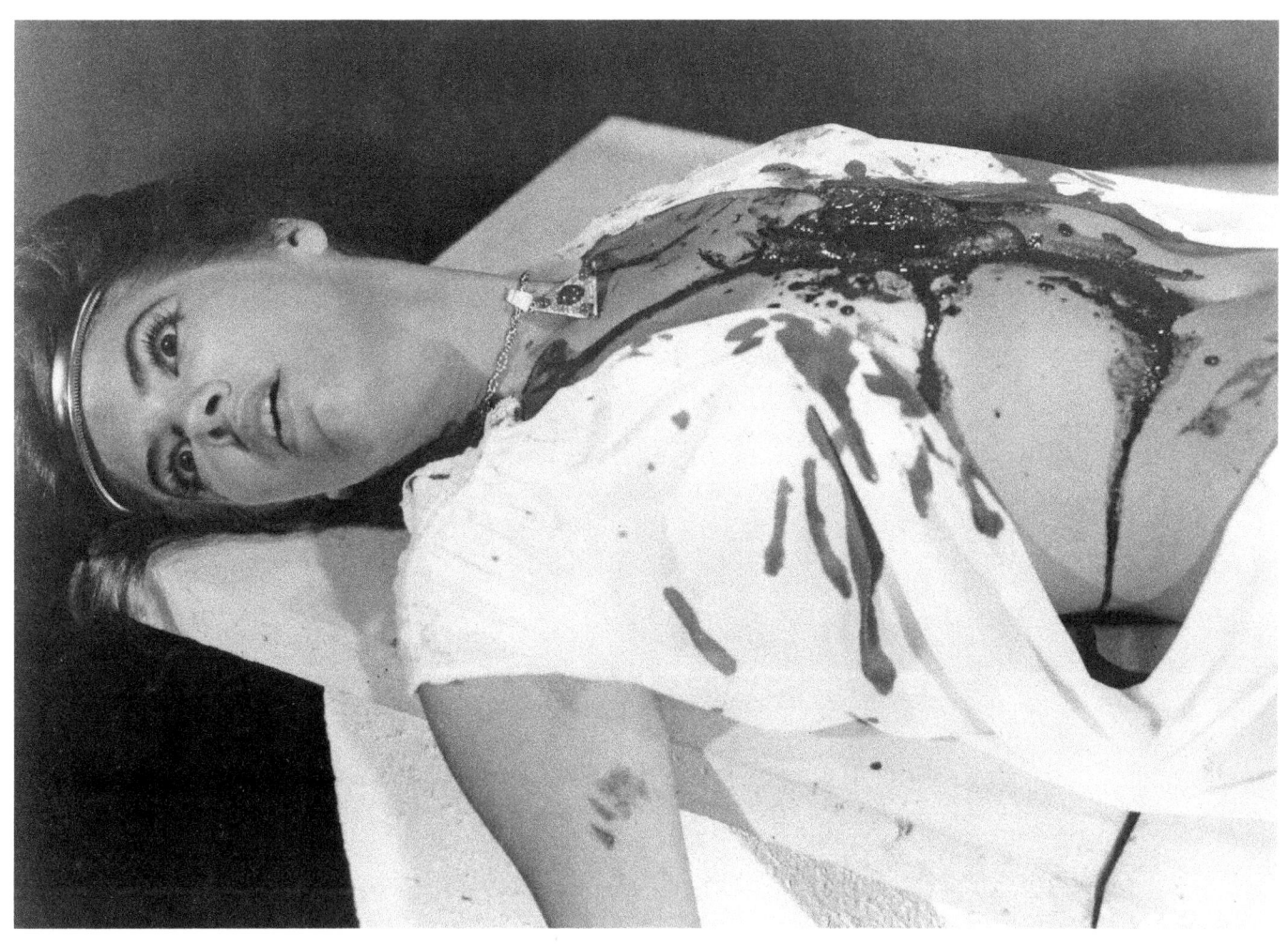

BLOOD FEAST
Production: USA, 1963
Director: Herschell Gordon Lewis
Category: Horror/Gore
Lewis invents the splatter movie with this outrageous, milestone offering; girls' limbs are cut off, tongues pulled out by the roots, eyeballs gouged out, brains removed, bodies flayed, etc etc, in lurid color and loving detail. A primitive masterpiece. **Blood Diner** (1987) was a pointless attempt at a "remake".

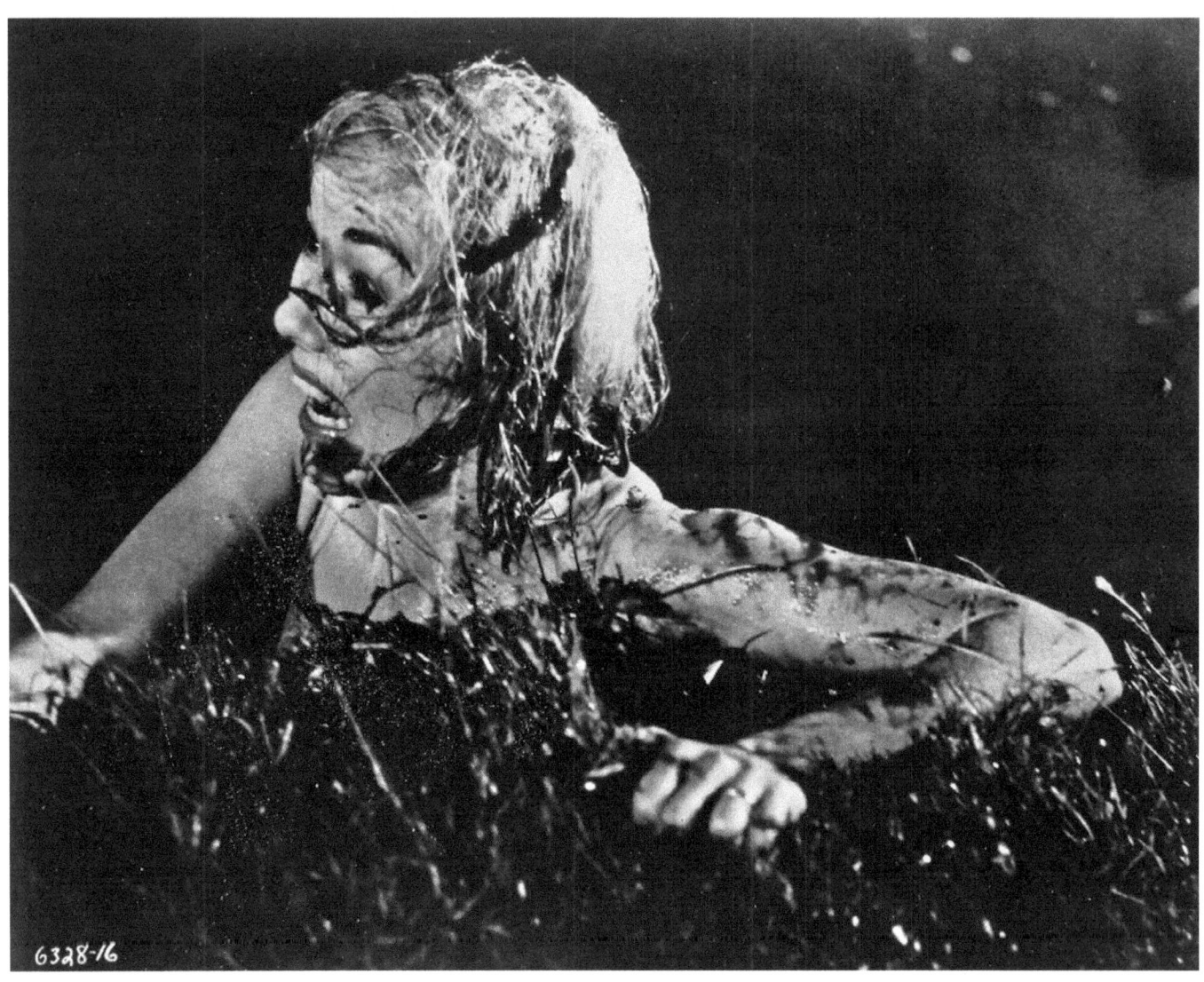

DEMENTIA 13
Production: USA, 1963
Director: Francis Ford Coppola
Category: Horror

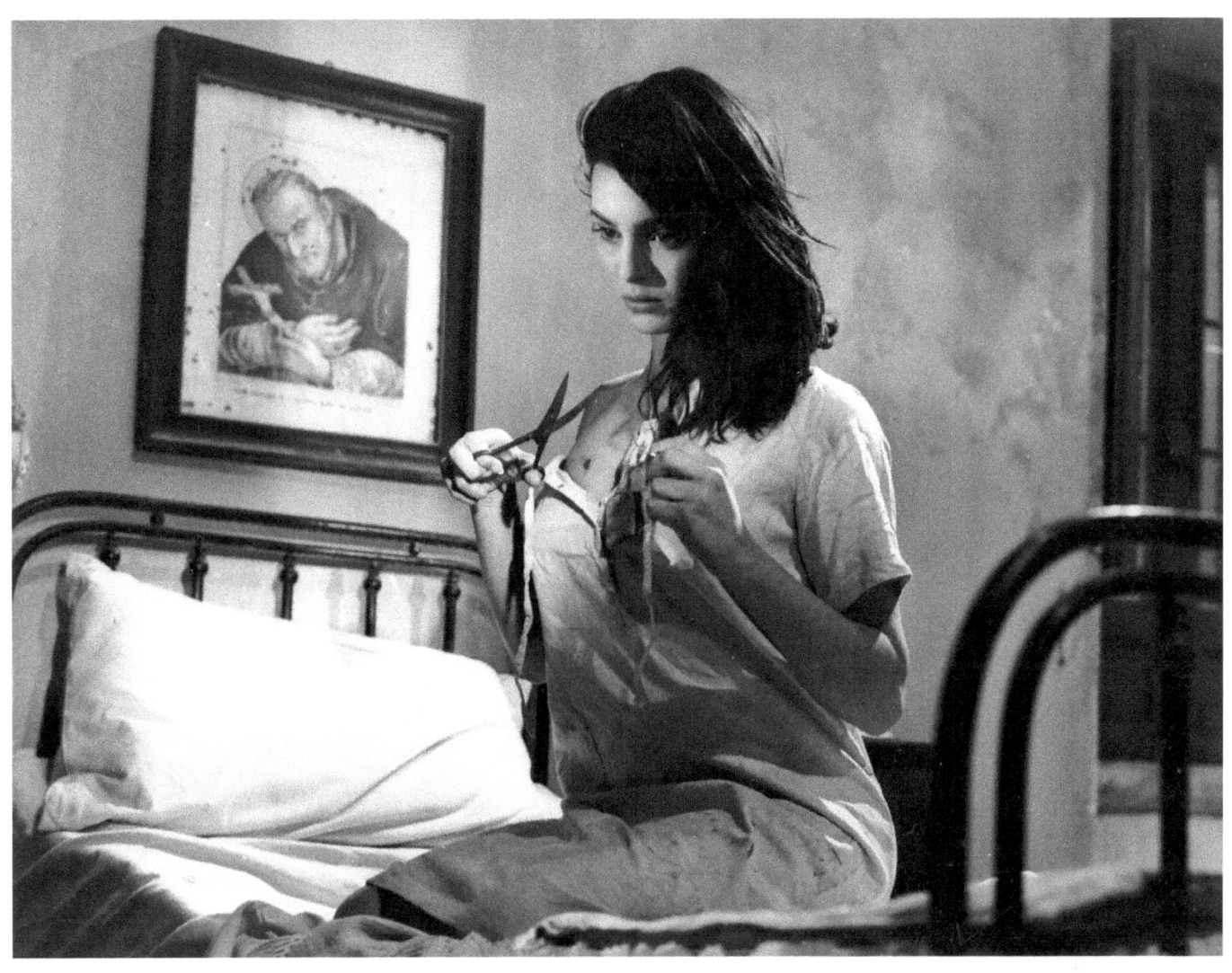

IL DEMONIO
("The Demon")
Production: Italy, 1963
Director: Brunello Rondi
Category: Horror

Daliah Lavi stars as a suspected witch/possessed woman. After attempts to exorcise her, she is killed by her fearful lover. Interesting for certain similarities in the exorcism scenes – speaking in tongues, crab-like physical contortions – to **The Exorcist,** which came a decade later.

DUNGEONS OF HORROR
Production: USA, 1963
Director: Pat Boyette
Alternative title: **Dungeon Of Harrow**
Category: Gothic Horror

Perhaps the earliest horror movie reference to the Marquis de Sade, in which one Count Lorente de Sade, an evil sadist, presides over a gloomy waterfront castle with his wife, the Countess. Representations of Sade have also appeared in several other minor horror features, including: **Waxwork** (1988), **Night Terrors** (1995), **Exotic House Of Wax** (1996), **Dead 2: The Skull Of Pain** (1997), and **Go To Hell** (1999). His supposed cranium also played the title role in the Amicus horror production **The Skull** (1965).

LA FRUSTA E IL CORPO
("The Whip And The Body")
Production: Italy, 1963
Director: Mario Bava
English release title: **Night Is The Phantom**
Category: Horror

Christopher Lee plays a revenant who savagely whips his lover (Dahlia Lavi) on a nightly basis, and whose penchant for sadistic sex previously led to the death of a servant girl. Bava's phantasmal colour schemata enhance the oneiric sex-violence to the point of delirium. **La Frusta E Il Corpo** belongs to that lurid corpus of early 60s Italian horror cinema in which sado-masochistic (not to mention necrophiliac) elements run riot, reaching a climax of sorts in Massimo Pupillo's **Il Boia Scarlatto** (1965).

THE HAUNTED PALACE
Production: USA, 1963
Director: Roger Corman
Category: Horror
Despite the title deriving from a poem by Edgar Allan Poe, this film is actually based on H.P. Lovecraft's brilliant novella *The Case Of Charles Dexter Ward*.

THE HAUNTING
Production: UK, 1963
Director: Robert Wise
Category: Horror

HORROR
Production: Italy, 1963
Director: Alberto De Martino
Category: Gothic Horror
English release title: **The Blancheville Monster**
A lesser-known addition to the Italian haunted castle/cursed family genre of early 60s horror movies, supposedly based on a story (unspecified, but probably "Fall Of The House Of Usher") by Edgar Allan Poe.

HOUSE OF THE DAMNED
Production: USA, 1963
Director: Maury Dexter
Category: Horror/Freaks
Classic exploitationer with real-life freaks in an old house; including a half-man, fat lady, and giant (Richard Kiel, future Bond movie star). A couple visiting an old mansion formerly owned by a sideshow boss become seeming victims of homicidal ghosts. The "ghosts" turn out to be a retinue of lost carnies, hiding out in the house since the showman's death.

THE INCREDIBLY STRANGE CREATURES WHO STOPPED LIVING AND BECAME CRAZY MIXED-UP ZOMBIES
Production: USA, 1963-64
Director: Ray Dennis Steckler
Alternative title: **Teenage Psycho Meets Bloody Mary**
Category: Horror
Steckler's notorious Z-movie used a carnival setting to tell its legendarily confused story about a gypsy fortune-teller with her own retinue of acid-scarred zombies, who hypnotizes a man (played by Steckler under the screen-name Cash Flagg) into committing a string of murders. The zombies finally break loose and kill everyone in sight. Billed as "the first monster musical", this unclassifiable absurdity is redeemed only by exquisite, saturated colour photography from Vilmos Zsigmond and Laszlo Kovacs, and remains most notable for lending its name to the innovative RE/Search tome *Incredibly Strange Films*.

LA INVASIÓN DE LOS VAMPIROS

("Invasion Of The Vampires")
Production: Mexico, 1963
Director: Miguel Morayta
Category: Horror
A sequel to Morayta's earlier **El Vampiro Sangriento**, continuing the struggles of the Cagliostro dynasty against the depraved vampire Count Frankenhausen.

KATARSIS

Production: Italy, 1963
Director: Giuseppe Veggezzi
Alternative title: **Sfida Al Diavolo**
Category: Horror
Another rare Italian 60s satanic horror movie, with one of numerous appearances by Christopher Lee in that genre, here playing Mephistopheles in a modern-day update of the Faust story. Set, as always, in a gothic castle, the film concerns a group of young people who set out to help man who has sold his soul to the Devil. It was filmed, like many others, in Odescalchi Castle near Rome. Lee, following his success in Hammer's **Dracula** (1958), returned to work in his native (on his mother's side) Italy in 1959, appearing in the more light-hearted **Tempi Duri Per I Vampiri**; he ended up making several other horror films there in the next few years, culminating with l **Castello Dei Morti Vivi** in 1964.

KISS OF THE VAMPIRE
Production: UK, 1963
Director: Don Sharp
Category: Horror

Hammer's third completed excursion into vampire cinema, **Kiss Of The Vampire** was the first to feature neither Peter Cushing nor Christopher Lee, and bravely eschewed all mention of the word "Dracula"; instead, we meet Dr. Ravna (Noel Willman), whose castle is the headquarters of a vampire circle in Bavaria, and his opponent Professor Zimmer (Clifford Evans). A young couple honeymooning in the forests foolishly accept Ravna's hospitality, and fall prey to the bloodsuckers. The bride is rescued by Zimmer's intervention, which leads to a swarm of avenging bats destroying the vampires. An aura of sexual disorder is established, right from the shocking opening shot of Zimmer driving a spade through his daughter's defiled body; his account of her ruination at the hands of Ravna clearly likens vampirism to a venereal disease. Intelligently directed by Don Sharp with deliberate utilisation of classically-trained actors, the film was a welcome return to increasingly familiar territory for Hammer.

LAS LUCHADORAS CONTRA EL MÉDICO ASESINO
("She-Wrestlers Versus The Killer Doctor")
Production: Mexico, 1963
Director: René Cardona
US release title: **Doctor Of Doom**
Category: Horror/Science Fiction

Cardona presents the first horror-wrestling movie to star female wrestlers, in this case Gloria Venus (Lorena Velázquez) and Golden Rubi (Elizabeth Campbell) who tangle with the mad doctor who killed Venus' sister in one of a series of underground brain transplants, which also resulted in the creaton of a half-ape, half-human monster. Cardona, Velázquez and Campbell quickly teamed up again for a sequel, the equally wild **Las Luchadoras Contra La Momia** (1964), released by Murray in 1965 as **Wrestling Women Vs. The Aztec Mummy**, followed by **Las Lobas Del Ring** (1965). The girls' last movie togther was Alfredo B. Crevenna's (non-wrestling) SF fantasy **El Planeta De Las Mujeres Invasoras** (1967, a sequel to his **Gigantes Planetarios**), and that same year Campbell played Golden Rubi for the last time in Cardona's **Las Mujeres Panteras** (with Ariadna Welter stepping into the role of Venus). Cardona's belated **Las Luchadoras Vs El Robot Asesino** (1969), featured neither Velázquez nor Campbell.

LA MALDICIÓN DE LA LLORONA
("Curse Of The Wailing Woman")
Production: Mexico, 1963
Director: Rafael Baledón
Category: Horror

One of the key films from the golden age of Mexican horror, in which a female descendent of the Wailing Woman enters a haunted mansion that houses the rotting remains of her ancestor. With a hideously disfigured acolyte and all the other prerequisites for a feast of gothic horror. Evoking an atmosphere similar to that achieved by Mario Bava in **La Maschera Del Demonio,** director Baledón has created a visceral experience replete with grotesque visual flourishes.

METEMPSYCHO
Production: Italy, 1963
Director: Antonio Boccaci
Category: Gothic Horror
Known in English as **Tomb Of Torture**, this Italian horror is not iquite on the level of works by Mario Bava, but scores some points for its Sadean atmosphere, a gothic castle setting, and a disfigured hunchback torturer. Boccaci's only film as director.

MONSTROSITY
Production: USA, 1963
Director: Joseph V. Mascelli
TV title: **The Atomic Brain**
Category: Horror/Science Fiction

A rich old woman, confined to a wheelchair, hires a scientist to transplant her brain into a sexy young body, using nuclear energy. She hires several maids for the purpose, but meanwhile the doctor is conducting experiments of his own in her basement; his creations include a feral hybrid, a female zombie and, best of all, a girl with the brain of a cat. Director Mascelli – also a cinematographer for Ray Dennis Steckler – has created his very own monster with this movie, a wild concoction of sleaze, medical mania, and deranged horror topped off by a contrapunctual voice-over.

PARQUE DE JUEGOS
("The Playground")
Production: Spain, 1963
Director: Pedro Olea
Category: Horror/Fantasy
16-minute adapatation of a Ray Bradbury short story, "The Playground", in which a man transposes personalities with his son in order to take his place on an evil, hellish playground charged with negative energy, where such creatures as vampires roam.

THE RAVEN
Production: USA, 1963
Director: Roger Corman
Category: Horror/Fantasy/Comedy
One of two films in Corman's Poe series, both from 1963, which took their title and a few words from a Poe poem but delivered a completely unrelated srory (the other being **The Haunted Palace**). **The Raven** gathers together horror icons Vincent Price, Boris Karloff and Peter Lorre in a tale of sorcery, betrayal and revenge, spoiled by a comic atmosphere. Thankfully, Corman would get serious again for his final two Poe derivatives, produced the following year.

ROSTRO INFERNAL
("Hell-Face")
Production: Mexico, 1963
Director: Alfredo B. Crevenna
US release title: **The Incredible Face Of Dr. B**
Category: Horror/Science Fiction

The first of two films by Crevenna concerning the depraved crimes of Count Brankovan, a mad scientist who seeks immortality by drinking the liquefied brains of his murder victims. In the sequel, **Huella Macabra** ("Mark Of The Macabre", also 1963), Brankovan rises from the tomb to pursue vengeance against his enemies, aided by his vampire son and a pair of albino zombies.

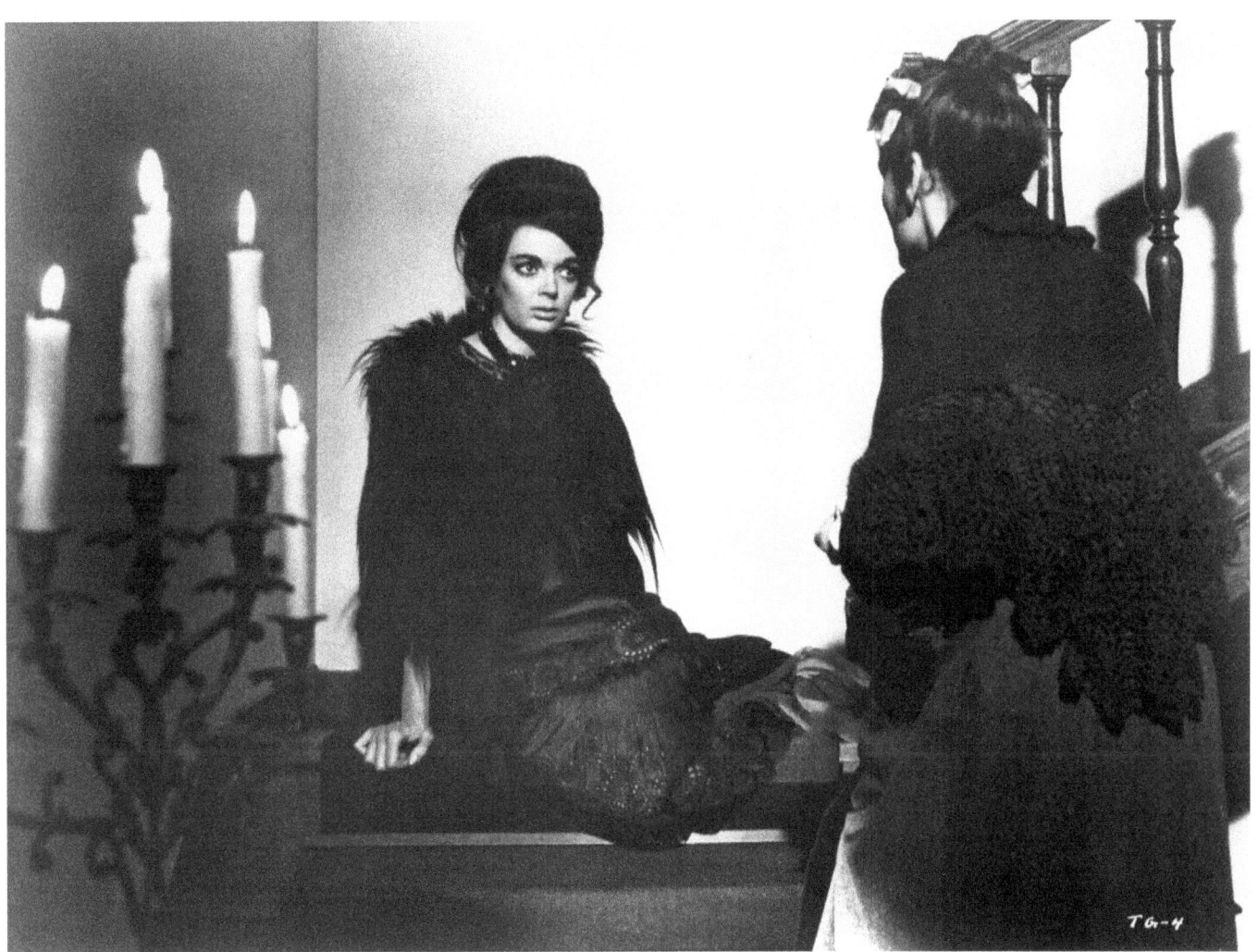

LO SPETTRO
("The Spectre")
Production: Italy, 1963
Director: Riccardo Freda
Category: Gothic Horror

One of the numerous Italian horror movies starring Barbara Steele, shot as a sequel of sorts to Freda's **Raptus**. Lo Spettro is another twisted psychological thriller, less perverse and delirious than its predecesor, but not without moments of gothic beauty and malevolence.

THE TERROR
Production: USA, 1963
Director: Roger Corman
Category: Horror

I TRE VOLTI DELLA PAURA
("The Three Faces Of Fear")
Production: Italy, 1963
Director: Mario Bava, Salvatore Billitteri
English release title: **Black Sabbath**
Category: Horror
Three tales of terror, the best of which is *The Vurdulak*, starring Boris Karloff. Said to be the inspiration for naming the quintessential horror-leaning heavy rock band of the 60s.

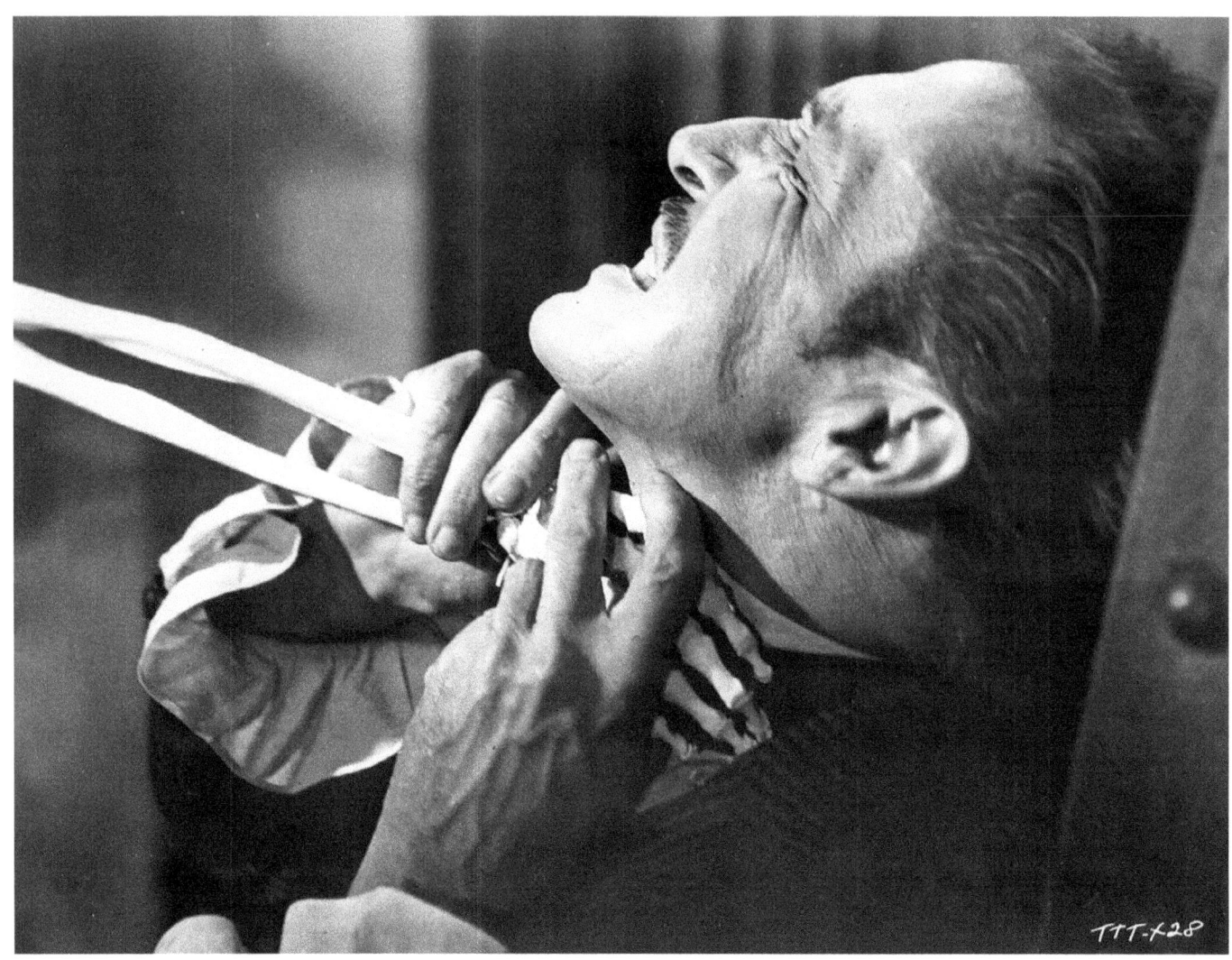

TWICE-TOLD TALES
Production: USA, 1963
Director: Sidney Salkow
Category: Horror
Borrowing the idea, format and leading man from Roger Corman's **Tales Of Terror**, but replacing Edgar Allan Poe with Nathaniel Hawthorne as source material, Salkow presents segments inspired by "Dr. Heidegger's Experiment" (1837), "Rappaccini's Daughter" (1844), and the gothic novel *The House Of The Seven Gables* (1851).

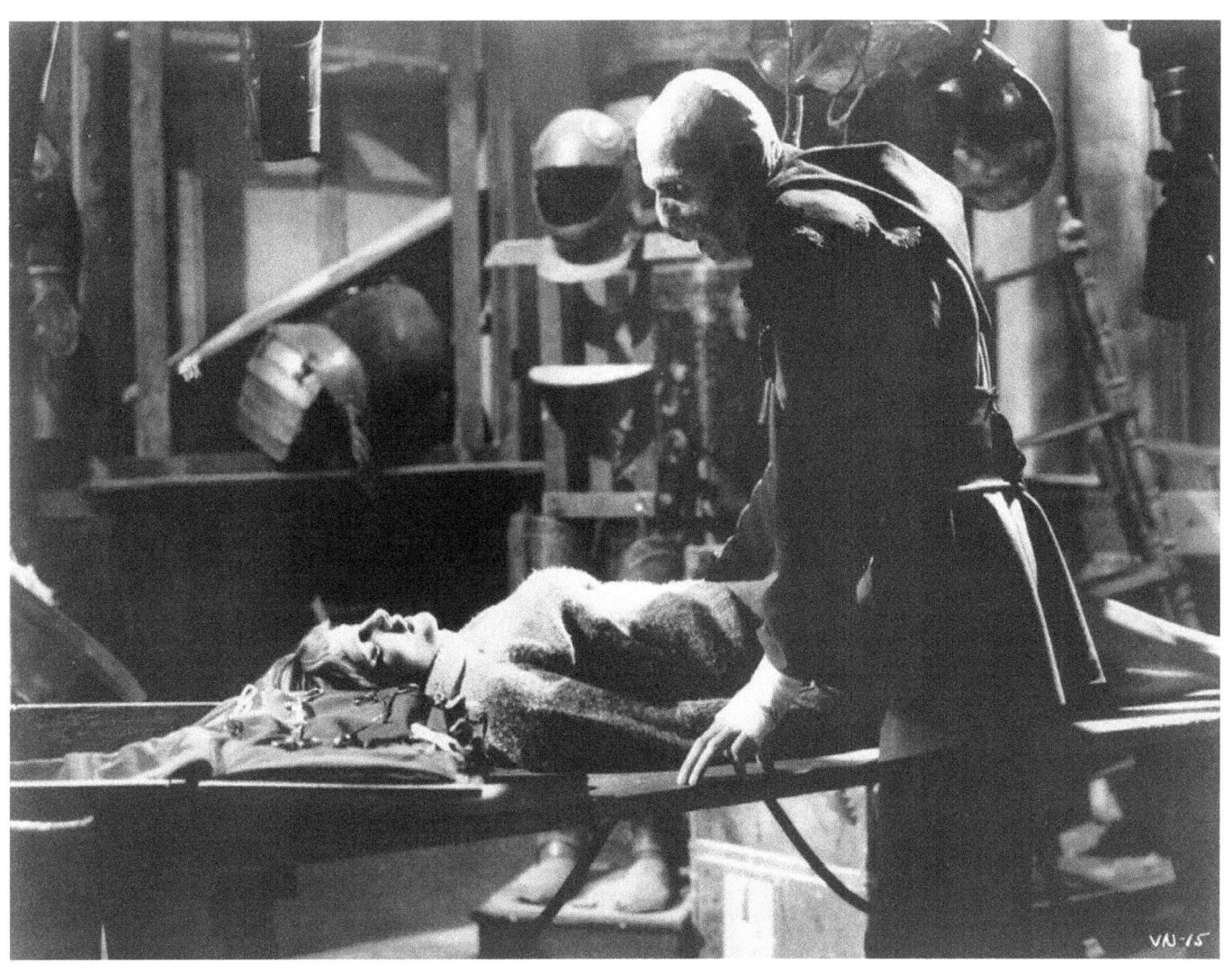

LA VERGINE DI NORIMBERGA
("The Virgin Of Nuremberg")
Production: Italy, 1963
Director: Antonio Margheriti
English release title: **Horror Castle**
Category: Gothic Horror

THE ADDAMS FAMILY
Production: USA, 1964-66
Director: Various
Category: Horror Comedy

The macabre cartoons of Charles Addams began appearing in *The New Yorker* in the 1930s, and were later reproduced in several book collections, including *Drawn And Quartered* (1942) and *Nightcrawlers* (1957). Based on his work, the **Addams Family** ABC TV series ran for 64 episodes of gothic absurdism, a killing joke at the expense of America – the Addams' mansion is a bastion of pseudo-European culture and sophistication amidst a sea of trash that occasionally laps at its gates before retreating in fear – repeated on a weekly basis. Clearly superior to its supposed rival, **The Munsters**, which worked on a more juvenile "monster mash" level.

THE BLACK TORMENT
Production: UK, 1964
Director: Robert Hartford-Davis
Category: Horror

Tigon production, a period ghost story in which the wife of a baronet investigates hauntings that are reported following the suicide of her husband's first bride. Gothic atmosphere and some striking spectral scenes elevate this otherwise mundane effort.

IL CASTELLO DEI MORTI VIVENTI
("The Castle Of The Living Dead")
Production: Italy, 1964
Director: Luciano Ricci, Lorenzo Sabatini
Category: Horror
A minor Italian horror film, most notable for Christopher Lee in the lead role of corpse-collector Count Drago, an early screen appearance by Donald Sutherland, and the participation as script-writer of Michael Reeves, the precocious young English director. There's also a cavorting dwarf, which makes any film more frightening with frissons of the uncanny. Reeves was allowed to direct part of the movie, warming up for his full debut with **La Sorella Di Satana** in 1966.

CURSE OF SIMBA
Production: UK, 1964
Director: Lindsay Shonteff
US release title: **Curse Of The Voodoo**
Category: Horror
A hunter who kills a sacred lion is cursed by an African tribesman. Despite the US title, the curse is not specified as deriving from voodoo, which is usually associated with Haiti. This was more accurately addressed in Joe Sarno's **Sin You Sinners** (1963), in which a mystic stripper uses the hypnotic powers of a Haitian amulet to retain her powers of sexual attraction and compel men to kill for her.

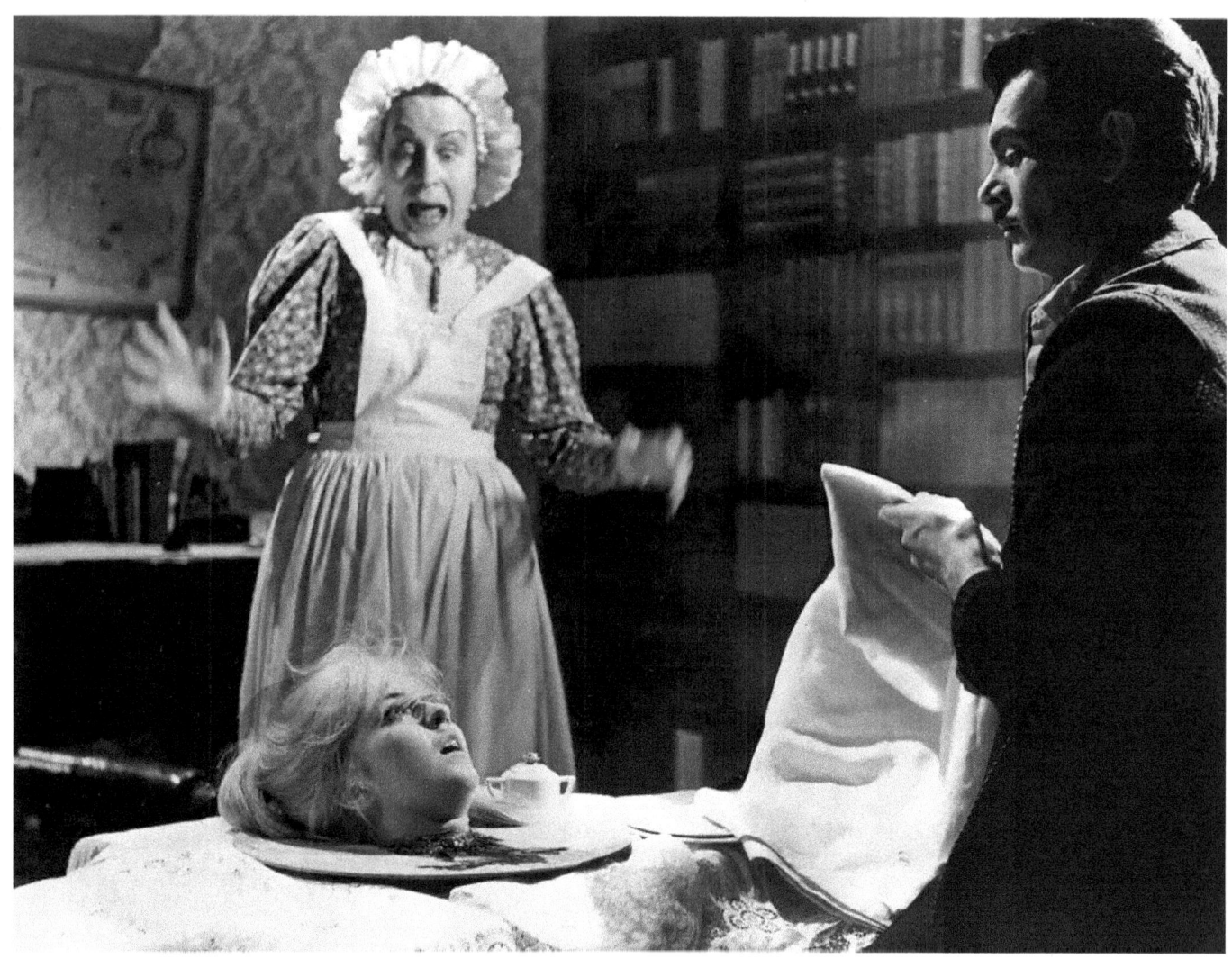

CURSE OF THE LIVING CORPSE
Production: USA, 1964
Director: Del Tenney
Category: Horror

CURSE OF THE MUMMY'S TOMB
Production: UK, 1964
Director: Michael Carreras
Category: Horror
Mummy films have always been among the weakest horror sub-genres, and this Hammer effort does little to prove otherwise. Only their original **The Mummy**, with Christopher Lee and Peter Cushing, and the final attempt **Blood From The Mummy's Tomb,** with Valerie Leon and trendy gore, retain much interest.

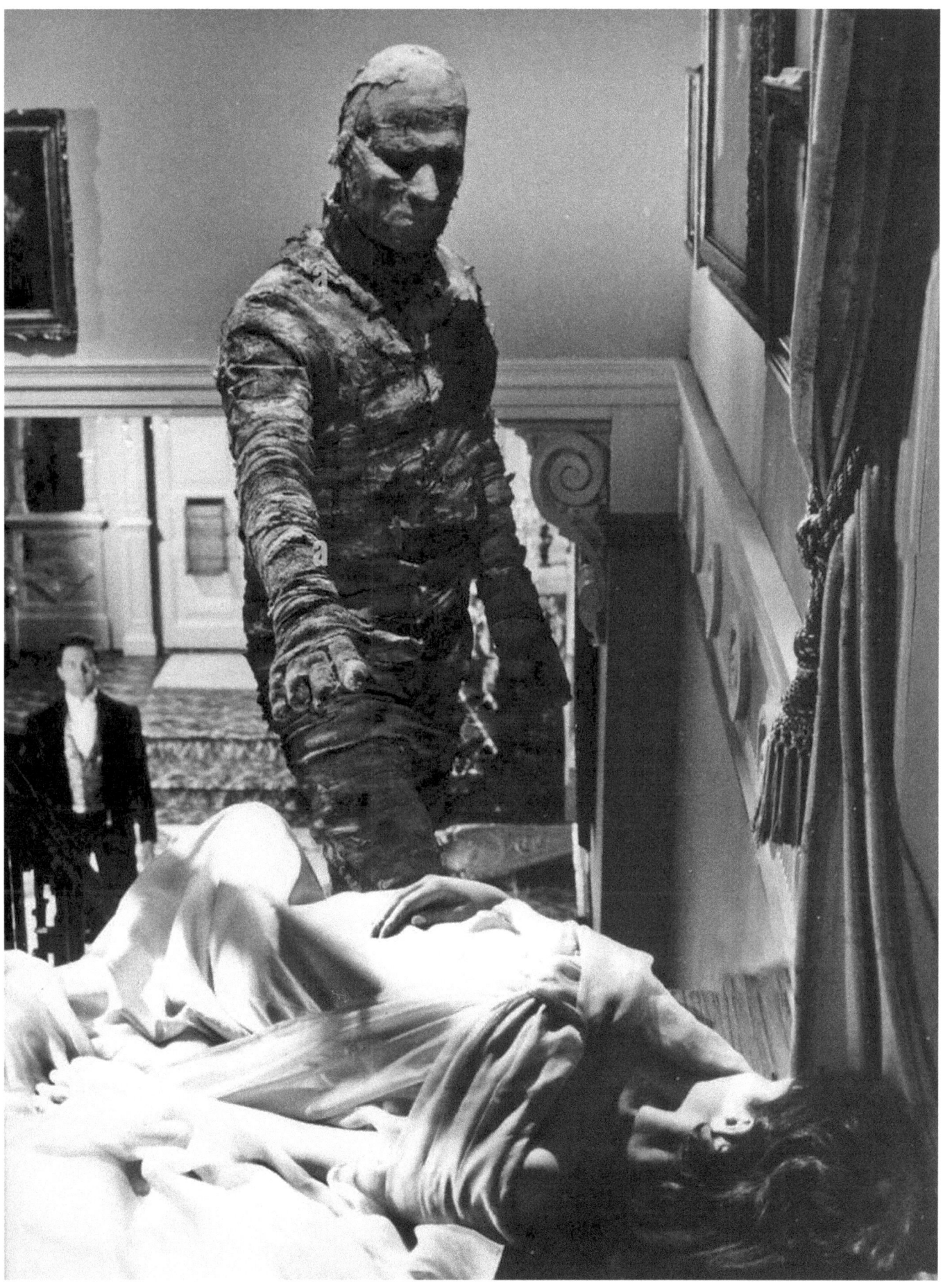

DANZA MACABRA
Production: Italy, 1964
Director: Antonio Marheriti
English release title: **Castle Of Blood**
Category: Horror
Another classic of Italian gothic horror starring Barbara Steele, this time as a deadly revenant. Remade by Margheriti in technicolor as **Nella Stretta Morsa Del Ragno** (1971), featuring Klaus Kinski as a demented Edgar Allan Poe.

THE DEVIL DOLL
Production: UK, 1964
Director: Lindsay Shonteff
Category: Horror

DEVIL WOLF OF SHADOW MOUNTAIN
Production: USA, 1964
Director: Gary Kent
Category: Horror/Western
Legendary horror-western which nobody seems to have seen and some think never even existed. Most likely it was announced, and test footage was shot, but then the project was shelved. In the film's original plot outline, a cowboy is infected with lycanthropy by drinking water from a wolf's paw-print, and photos of a supposed transformation sequence appeared in issue 9 of the magazine *Mad Monsters*. Other shadowy, unseen films of legend from the same era include **The Insane Demons Of Topanga Canyon** and **The Demon From Devil's Lake**.

DOCTOR TERROR'S HOUSE OF HORRORS
Production: UK, 1964
Director: Freddie Francis
Category: Horror

The first of the several horror anthologies produced by Amicus, with Peter Cushing as Dr. Schreck, a tarot-reader on a train who reveals fatal futures to his fellow passengers, played out in various episodes. These include Christopher Lee (haunted by a severed hand), Donald Sutherland (tricked by a vampire), and cult British DJ Alan Freeman (menaced by a killer vine). Schreck turns out to be Death, and the train is the Hell-bound express. For this debut horror production, which was eventually released in 1965, Amicus (formed in 1962) had clearly targeted the top stars, and one of the leading directors, in the British cinema of terror and the supernatural, perhaps in the hope of rivalling Hammer. The company's next anthology film would be **Torture Garden** in 1967.

EVIL OF FRANKENSTEIN
Production: UK, 1964
Director: Freddie Francis
Category: Horror

Third in the Hammer franchise. Baron Frankenstein (Peter Cushing once again) is on the run from yet another band of outraged villagers, when he somehow comes across one of his earlier creations, a semi-human monster (played by Kiwi Kingston) that has been preserved in a glacier. Recruiting a mesmerist to help reactivate its damaged brain (the rest of the creature responding to a charge of electricity), the Baron soon finds himself competing for control of the thing, which is sent by the hypnotist on some errands of theft and murder. Even when Frankenstein retrieves his creation, he is unable to stop it getting drunk on brandy and then consuming an agonising dose of chloroform; both the Baron and the creature seemingly perish in a fire. Kingston's make-up here closely resembles Boris Karloff's for the first time, and the plot seems to be a deliberate throwback to the Universal days – but nothing in the film is truly memorable.

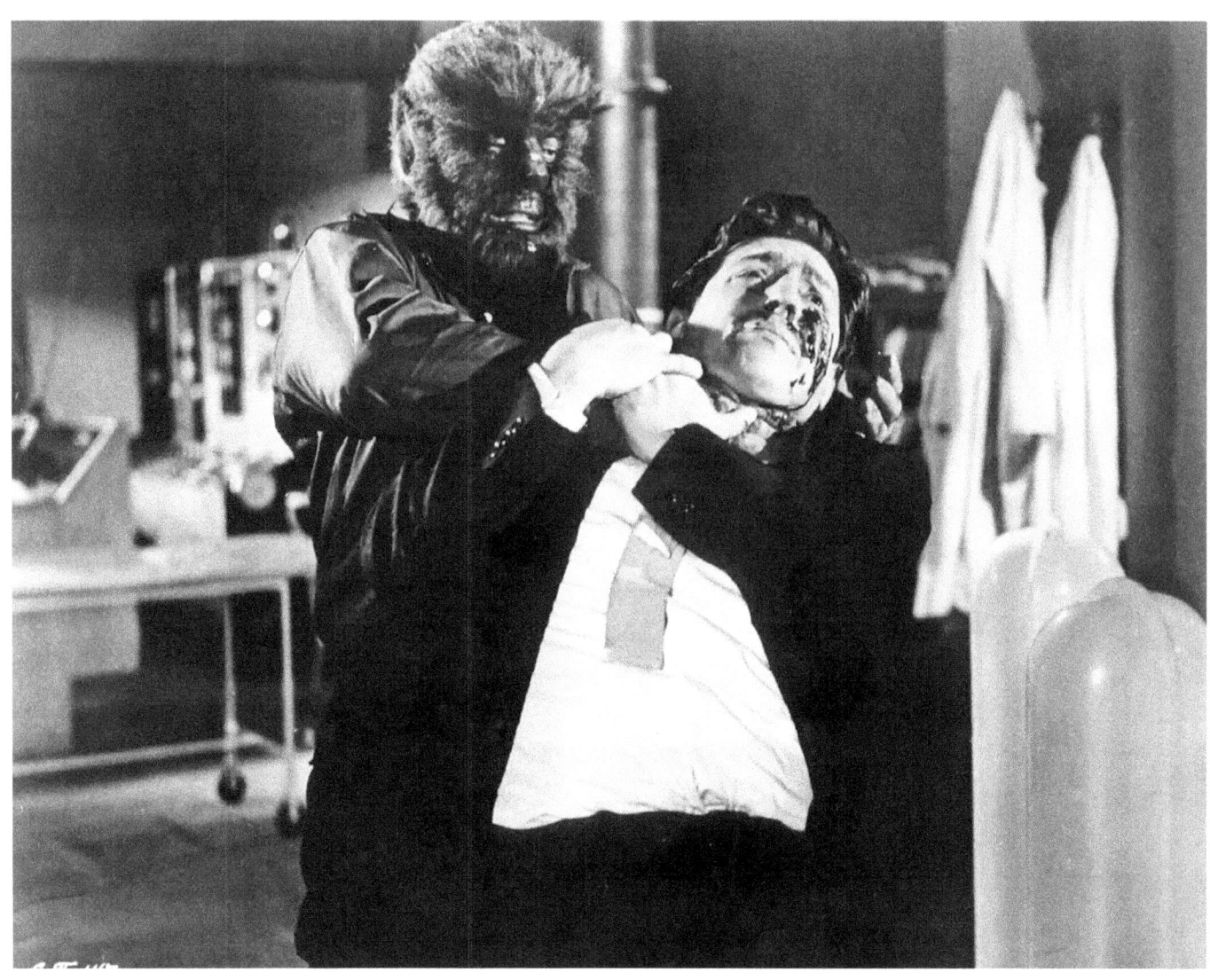

FACE OF THE SCREAMING WEREWOLF
Production: USA, 1964
Director: Jerry Warren
Category: Horror/Western

Warren, a Z-movie hack responsible for such trash horror items as **Teenage Zombies** (1959), was best-known for cannibalizing other directors' films and reassembling them into new, malformed and monstrous travesties. **Face Of The Screaming Werewolf** is a prime example, in which Warren took footage from two Mexican horror movies – **La Momia Azteca** (Rafael Portillo, 1957) and **La Casa Del Terror** (Gilberto Martínez Solares, 1960) – and spliced it all together with additional sequences which he shot himself. The werewolf, taken from **La Casa Del Terror**, is played by Lon Chaney, Jr, reprising for the last time the role which brought him fame in the 1940s. Warren also did an extensive reshoot of **La Momia Azteca** by itself, butchering it and retitling it **Attack Of The Mayan Mummy** for US TV. Another Warren chop-job from that same year was **Curse Of The Stone Hand**, which lifted and spliced footage from two elegant Chilean horror movies from 1945, Carlos Schlieper's **La Casa Está Vacía** and Carlos Hugo Christensen's **La Dama De La Muerte**, plus new scenes filmed with John Carradine. And so, as if in a trance, Warren involuntarily spewed forth the ectoplasm of a bizarre form of collage-film, a sewer-level manifestation of the Surrealist notion of objective chance.

DER FLUCH DER GRÜNEN AUGEN
("Curse Of The Green Eyes")
Production: Germany/Yugoslavia, 1964
Director: Ákos Ráthonyi
English release title: **Cave Of The Living Dead**
Category: Horror/Crime
A mixture of crime mystery and vampire horror with some gothic flourishes, though fairly tame with regard to shocks or skin.

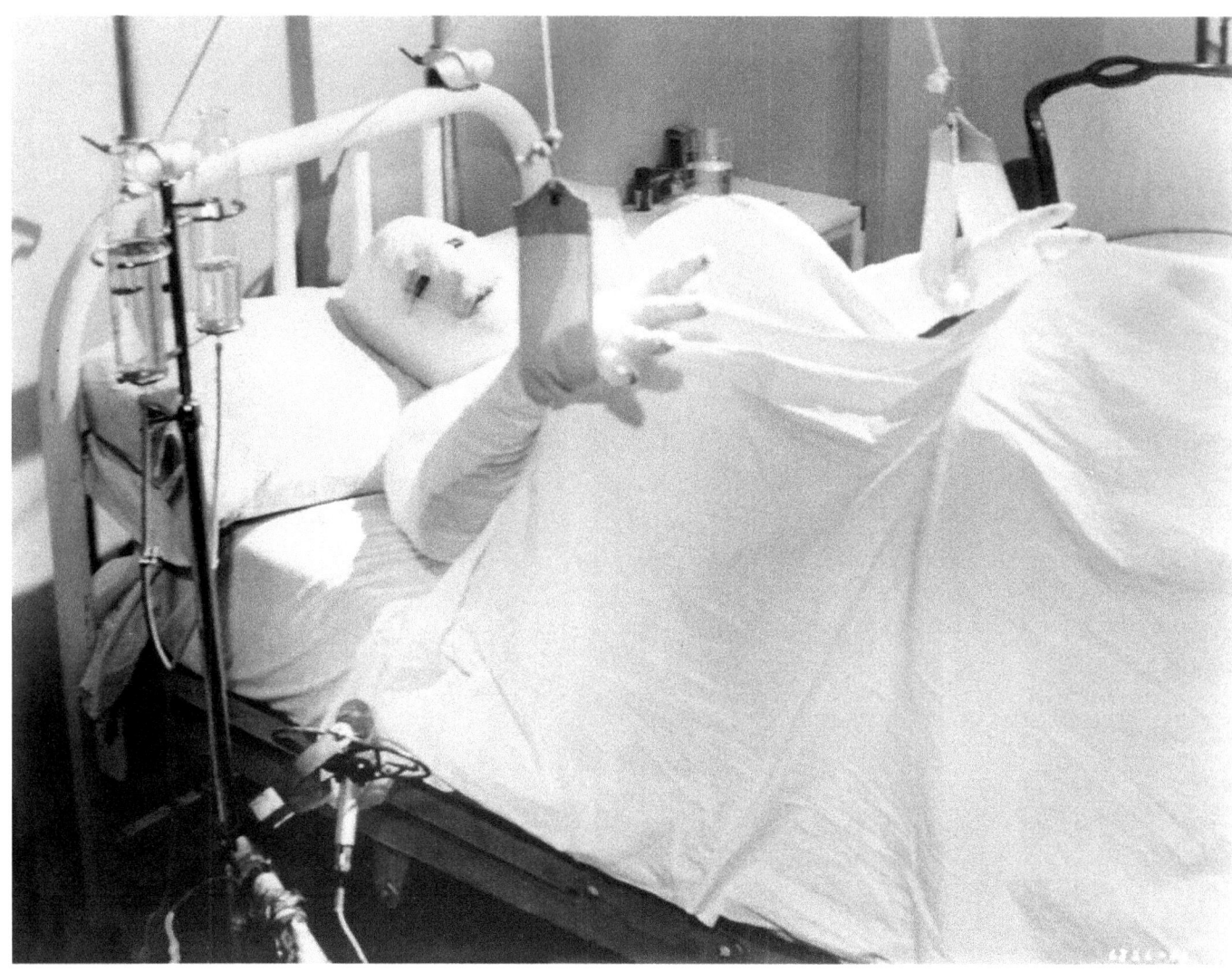

FUEGO
("Fire")
Production: Spain, 1964
Director: Julio Koll
English release title: **Pyro... The Thing Without A Face**
Category: Horror

THE GORGON
Production: UK, 1964
Director: Terence Fisher
Category: Horror
Presumably having covered every traditional monster angle, Hammer next turned to Greek mythology and came up with **The Gorgon**. Translating the action to Transylvania, the story tells of villagers being literally petrified by the Gorgon Medusa, a monstrous female with hissing, writhing serpents in her hair. She turns out to have possessed the beautiful Carla (Barbara Shelley, who was to the British horror film what Barbara Steele had become to the Italian), and to be in league with a brain surgeon, Namaroff (Peter Cushing). Christopher Lee does the honours as Meister, the university professor who sets out to liberate the villagefolk from evil,

finally cutting off her head like a latter-day Perseus. Despite Shelley's willingness to play both roles (even with live snakes in her hair), the Gorgon was finally portrayed by Prudence Hyman. Again directed by Terence Fisher, this was an uneven but entertaining attempt to try out a new creature, marked by its bleak ending.

HORROR AT PARTY BEACH
Production: USA, 1964
Director: Del Tenney
Category: Horror/Musical

The popularity of teen "beach party" movies, which started with William Asher's AIP production **Beach Party** in 1963, led not only to sequels such as **Muscle Beach Party** and **Bikini Beach** (both 1964), but also to daft hybrids such as **Horror At Party Beach**. This experiment culminated bizarrely with Vincent Price in **Dr. Goldfoot And The Bikini Machine** (1965) and Boris Karloff in **The Ghost In The Invisible Bikini** (1966), after which the only way for the explosive, fleeting "beach party" genre was downhill into obscurity.

KAIDAN
("Ghost Stories")
Production: Japan, 1964
Director: Masaki Kobayashi
English release title: **Kwaidan**
Category: Horror

Kaidan, one of the best-known of all Japanese films in the West, consists of four episodes based on traditional ghost stories originally translated by Lafcadio Hearn. In *Kurokami* ("The Black Hair") a samurai beds his wife only to find her a rotting corpse by morning; in *Yuki-Onna* ("The Snow Woman") a beautiful spectre lures men to a frozen death; in *Miminashi Hoichi No Hanashi* ("Hoichi The Earless") a musician is painted with runes to ward off ghosts, but his ears, left uncovered, are ripped off; and in *Chawan No Naka* ("In A Cup Of Tea") a samurai sees a phantom's face in a teacup. All the pieces are visually elegant, haunting works. The *Yuki-Onna* episode was sometimes excised and screened separately, especially outside Japan, to make the film's 183-minute duration more manageable.

KULAY DUGO ANG GABI
("Night Is The Colour Of Blood")
Production: Philippines/USA, 1964
Director: Gerardo De Leon
English release title: **The Blood Drinkers**
Category: Horror
Partly shot in colour, partially in tinted black-and-white (simply due to budgetary restrictions), this is a very unusual vampire movie reminiscent of Mexican horror cinema with its retinue of weird characters and its profoundly irrational narrative. De Leon made a sequel, **Creatures Of Evil,** in 1966.

I LUNGHI CAPELLI DELLA MORTE
("The Long Hair Of Death")
Production: Italy, 1964
Director: Antonio Margheriti
Category: Horror

THE MASQUE OF THE RED DEATH
Production: UK/USA, 1964
Director: Roger Corman
Category: Horror

Corman unfurls a tableau of absolute evil and corruption set in a sundered castle divorced from civilisation by plague and war, sourced from Edgar Allan Poe. With cinematography by Nicolas Roeg, the film features amazing colour shifts as the accursed action moves from chamber to chamber, building to its climax of mass extermination. Sadly, key scenes of a black magic ritual were banned by the moronic British censor. Corman also interwove the Poe story "Hop-Frog", with dwarf actor Skip Martin as the vengeful court jester who burns his tormentors alive. Overall, **Masque Of The Red Death** represents the apex of Corman's Poe series, with constant leading man Vincent Price as the devil-worshipping Prince Prospero presiding over a domain of cruelty, lust, madness and death which ultimately surpasses the rites of Bergman's **Det Sjunde Inseglet** in the annals of Grim Reaper cinema.

IL MOSTRO DELL'OPERA
("Monster Of The Opera")
Production: Italy, 1964
Director: Renato Polselli
Category: Horror

THE NAKED WITCH
Production: USA, 1964
Director: Larry Buchanan
Category: Horror
A college student is investigating the history of withcraft in a small Texas town with a populace of German descent; he unwittingly resurrects a malefic witch. Not to be confused with Andy Milligan's **The Naked Witch,** shot in 1967.

THE NIGHT WALKER
Production: USA, 1964
Director: William Castle
Category: Horror

One of two collaborations between Castle and scriptwriter Robert Bloch (the other was **Strait-Jacket**) that stand as the delirious pinnacle of the director's series of experimental horror movies. Whereas **Strait-Jacket** starred Joan Crawford, **The Night Walker** has Barbara Stanwyck in the lead role as a hysterical pyrophobe haunted by the living corpse of her blind, disfigured husband. A standard murder/blackmail plot is transformed into a paranoiac-critical eye-funeral with psychotronic music, a surrealistic haunted chapel of mannequins, an inpenetrable cycle of dreams within nightmares within dreams, and everything centring maniacally around a gaping hole that looms like a vulva leading into the very bowels of Hell. This is Castle's vertiginous masterpiece.

ONIBABA
("Old Devil Woman")
Production: Japan, 1964
Director: Kaneto Shindo
English release title: **The Hole**
Category: Horror

Kaneto Shindo's **Onibaba** is a devastating "horror" movie motivated by erotic compulsion and sexual jealousy. In feudal Japan, a middle-aged woman and her daughter-in-law are marsh-dwellers, scavenging from dead *samurai* to make ends meet. They sleep topless. Fearing her husband killed at war, the girl commences an affair with his comrade Hachi, who now lives nearby. Their crazed lust is evoked in beautiful moonlit shots, soundtracked by thunderous *kodo* drums, as they rush through the tall reeds to meet and consummate their passion. In the midst of this psychogeographical nightscape lies the hole itself, a repository for the looted corpses, resembling a monstrous vagina as we view it from above. Jealousy and fear of abandonment spur the elder woman to desperate measures. She kills a passing *samurai* and tears off his demonic warmask, revealing a hideously disfigured face beneath. She wears the mask by night, scaring the girl away from her trysts with

Hachi, until finally it becomes stuck fast to her face. In a harrowing scene of primal violence, her daughter-in-law smashes on the mask with a hammer, relishing every blow, until it finally splits away to reveal the mother-in-law's face as badly scarred as the *samurai*'s. By oppressing sexuality, she has become as one with those who oppressed her, the hated *samurai*, and her only recourse is to plunge headfirst into the hole itself in a frenzied climax of pandemoniac proportion. Shindo's other great horror film was **Kuroneko** (1968).

SPIDER BABY
Production: USA, 1964
Director: Jack Hill
Category: Horror

Jack Hill's outlandish **Spider Baby** presents the Merrye family, a demented, inbred brood suffering from their own indigenous illness, Merrye's Syndrome. The chief symptom of this affliction appears to be mental regression to the level of infancy, accompanied by homicidal urges and cannibalism. The family consists of Elizabeth (Beverly Washburn), a grown women who dresses and behaves like an eleven-year-old; Virginia (Jill Banner), the Spider Baby of the title who believes she is a spider and eats flies; and Ralph (Sid Haig), a bald sub-infantile freak. They are watched over by faithful chauffeur Bruno, played by Lon Chaney Jr (who also sings the title tune). When two distant relatives turn up with their lawyer to try and claim the family mansion for themselves, the scene is set for a grotesque display replete with greed, mental and physical disintegration, cannibalism, rape and murder, which is nonetheless saved, by dint of its primitive sensibilities, from being cynically gratuitous. More seriously deranged and dangerous than the Femm family from Whale's **Old Dark House**, though still with an edge of profoundly black humour to their antics, the Merryes seem to anticipate the ultimate degenerates of Tobe Hooper's **Texas Chainsaw Massacre**.

THE TOMB OF LIGEIA
Production: UK/USA, 1964
Director: Roger Corman
Category: Horror

The last, and one of the most interesting (though least-seen) of Corman's Poe cycle, **The Tomb Of Ligeia** was filmed in the English countryside, prompting director Corman to break his own avowed maxim of set-bound artificiality, maintained in all the previous entries.

WITCHCRAFT
Production: UK, 1964
Director: Don Sharp
Category: Horror

Lon Chaney Jr. – by then in the throes of terminal alcoholism, and looking it – plays a Morgan Whitlock, a warlock whose family of Devil-worshippers has been locked in a feud with the Lanier family for nearly four hundred years, after they buried alive Vanessa Whitlock, a sexy Devil's witch. Vanessa's corpse is disturbed when the present-day Laniers bulldoze the Whitlock family cemetery, and she returns to wreak vengeance. It all ends with in-fighting between Vanessa (in a grotesque performance by Yvette Rees) and her descendent Amy Whitlock, who has been initiated into witchhood but turns her back on the Devil to seek redemption, and the entire family of Satanists are finally consumed in a conflagration. **Witchcraft** is a prime example of the "vengeful witch" sub-genre, which frequently features the sins of the fathers being punished by the Devil's tribunal, and remains one of the best Satanic films produced in the UK.

ZOMBIE
Production: USA, 1964
Director: Del Tenney
Category: Horror/Western
This old b/w zombie effort, long unreleased, was salvaged by Jerry Gross in 1971 and retitled **I Eat Your Skin** in order to form a double bill with his production of David Durston's **I Drink Your Blood** (originally titled **Phobia**).

OTOKO NO MONSHO
("The Crest Of A Man")
Production: Japan, 1963
Director: Hideo Sasai
Category: Yakuza

THE CHAIR
Production: USA, 1963
Director: Robert Drew
Category: Documentary/Capital Punishment
Compelling and intelligent real-life documentary on a hearing to decide whether or not a black convict will win a last-minute reprieve from the electric chair; preparations for the execution are cut with desperate court scenes, building to a taut climax with the delivery of the judge's verdict. With photography and editing by Richard Leacock and D.A. Pennebaker, **The Chair** is a classic example of Direct Cinema, the American documentary movement which derived much inspiration from the "Candid-Eye" work done by Michel Brault and Pierre Perrault for the National Film Board of Canada.

THE COOL WORLD
Production: USA, 1963
Director: Shirley Clarke
Category: Juvenile Delinquency/Gangs
Clarke's follow-up to her controversial **The Connection** was another study in urban drug culture and disaffection, this time focusing on Harlem gangs. Shot on location, the film shows black youths addicted to drugs, dealing drugs, and buying guns,

some of them as young as fourteen. The roles are acted, but mostly by locals, based on real life cases, and under semi-improvised conditions. An example of the docudrama, produced by Frederick Wiseman who would later shoot his own brand of direct cinema, starting with **Titicut Follies** in 1966.

LA DONNA SCIMMIA
("The Ape Woman")
Production: Italy, 1963
Director: Marco Ferreri
Category: Freakshows

A roadshow huckster – who makes money touring slide-shows of naked African natives – passes off a hirsute woman as a true feral hybrid, after discovering her in a poorhouse. He eventually marries and impregnates her to stop her leaving; when she dies in child-birth, he simply uses her corpse, and that of the deformed baby, as an exhibit. Based on the real-life story of "Gorilla Woman" Julia Pastrana (born Mexico 1832), a hypertrichosis (excessive body hair) sufferer whose corpse was mummified by husband/promotor Theodore Lent and toured around Europe in a glass coffin.

ECCO
("Behold")
Production: Italy, 1963
Director: Gianni Proia
Category: Mondo
Combining footage taken from his earlier film **World By Night 2** (1962) with new material, director Proia attempts to go one better than **Mondo Cane** in the outrage stakes. Scenes include self-mutilation, a reindeer castration, and a blood-drenched Grand-Guignol performance. **Ecco** was re-edited and released in America by Lee Frost and Bob Cresse, the infamous exploitation movie duo whose work would find its apogee of notoriety with the later **Love Camp Seven**.

EINER FRISST DEN ANDEREN
("One Devours The Other")
Production: Germany/Italy, 1963-64
Director: Ray Nazarro, Gustav Gavrin & Richard E. Cunha
English release title: **Dog Eat Dog**
Category: Crime
A very strange, cult heist movie starring Cameron Mitchell and Jayne Mansfield as thieves; Mansfield plays Darlene, who is seen writhing orgasmically, half-naked, on

a bed covered in money; she also gets involved in a cat-fight and dances a lot. The film plays out on a strange secluded island, presided over by a crazy old woman and her bald servant, and features a series of bizarre murders. Probably Jayne's weirdest film, although she would be involved in several more as, no longer required by Hollywood, she gravitated to cheap Euro productions.

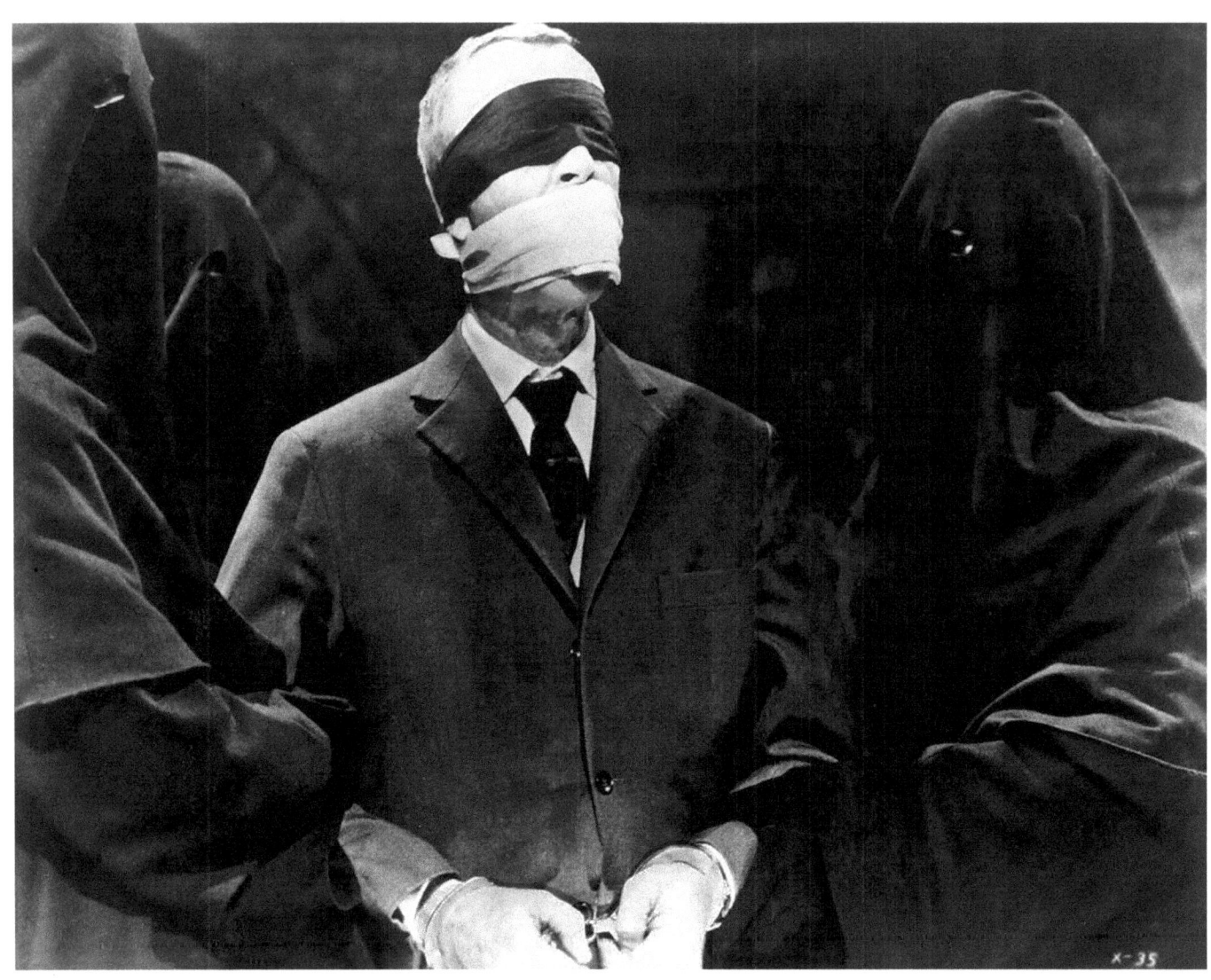

DER HENKER VON LONDON
("The London Headsman")
Production: Germany, 1963
Director: Edwin Zbonek
English release title: **The Mad Executioners**
Category: Krimi/Horror

Inspired by the huge success of Rialto's ongoing series of Edgar Wallace *grüselkrimis*, rival company CCC (Central Cinema Company) had the inspiration to hire the dead author's son, Bryan Edgar Wallace, to collaborate on a competing strand of macabre horror-mysteries. The first fruit of this project was **Das Geheimnis Der Schwarzen Koffer** (1961). **Der Henker Von London**, based on Bryan Edgar Wallace's own novel *The White Carpet*, concerns a clandestine group of hooded vigilantes, who operate outside the law and pass their own death sentences on criminals; meanwhile, a deranged serial killer is decapitating young women and using the heads in bizarre medical experiments. Complete with atmospheric, fog-bound London locations, **Der Henker Von London** showcases a more lurid tone than its Rialto rivals – such as the same year's **Der Zinker** ("The Squealer") – and this would persist throughout the ensuing productions. The best of these included **Der Würger Von Schloß Blackmoor** (1963), **Das Phantom Von Soho** (1964), and **Das Ungeheuer Von London-City** (1964), inspired by Jack the Ripper.

JUDEX
Production: France, 1963
Director: Georges Franju
Category: Crime
Franju's tribute to the great French crime serial from 1915 and its director, Louis Feuillade.

LORD OF THE FLIES
Production: UK, 1963
Director: Peter Brook
Category: Violence
A luminous vision of William Golding's allegory of civilization devolving into savagery, involving two tribes of children stranded on a remote island. Brilliantly updated, with a political edge, in Kinji Fukasaku's ultra-violent **Battle Royale** some three decades later.

MANIAC
Production: UK, 1963
Director: Michael Carreras
Category: Mania

A companion-piece of sorts to Hammer's other 1963 psycho movie, **Paranoaic**, **Maniac** was directed by company executive Carreras himself from another Jimmy Sangster script. An American artist in France (Kerwin Matthews) falls in love with a young woman but is seduced by her step-mother and persuaded to help her father to escape from a lunatic asylum. Some very bizarre scenes culminate in a typical Sangster surprise ending.

NIHON ZANKOKU MONOGATARI
("Cruel Stories From Japan")
Production: Japan, 1963
Director: Nobuo Nakagawa, Haku Komori & Ten Takahashi
Category: Mondo

Narrated by Teru Miyata, and including underwater footage shot by Eishin Osaki, **Cruel Stories From Japan** was the first major mondo movie produced in that country. As the title suggests, it has a sadistic focus on pain and blood-letting; scenes include hunting, killing and butchering animals (including a monkey's brains being scooped out), tattooing, surgical procedures, and physical trauma/death. Of the directors, Nakagawa was already renowned for a series of grotesque, surrealistic horror films; Komori would become a purveyor of sleazy *ero-guro* sex films such as the misogynistic **Gokuhi: Onna Gomon** ("Top Secret: Female Torture", 1968); and Takahashi appears to have few other screen accomplishments to his name.

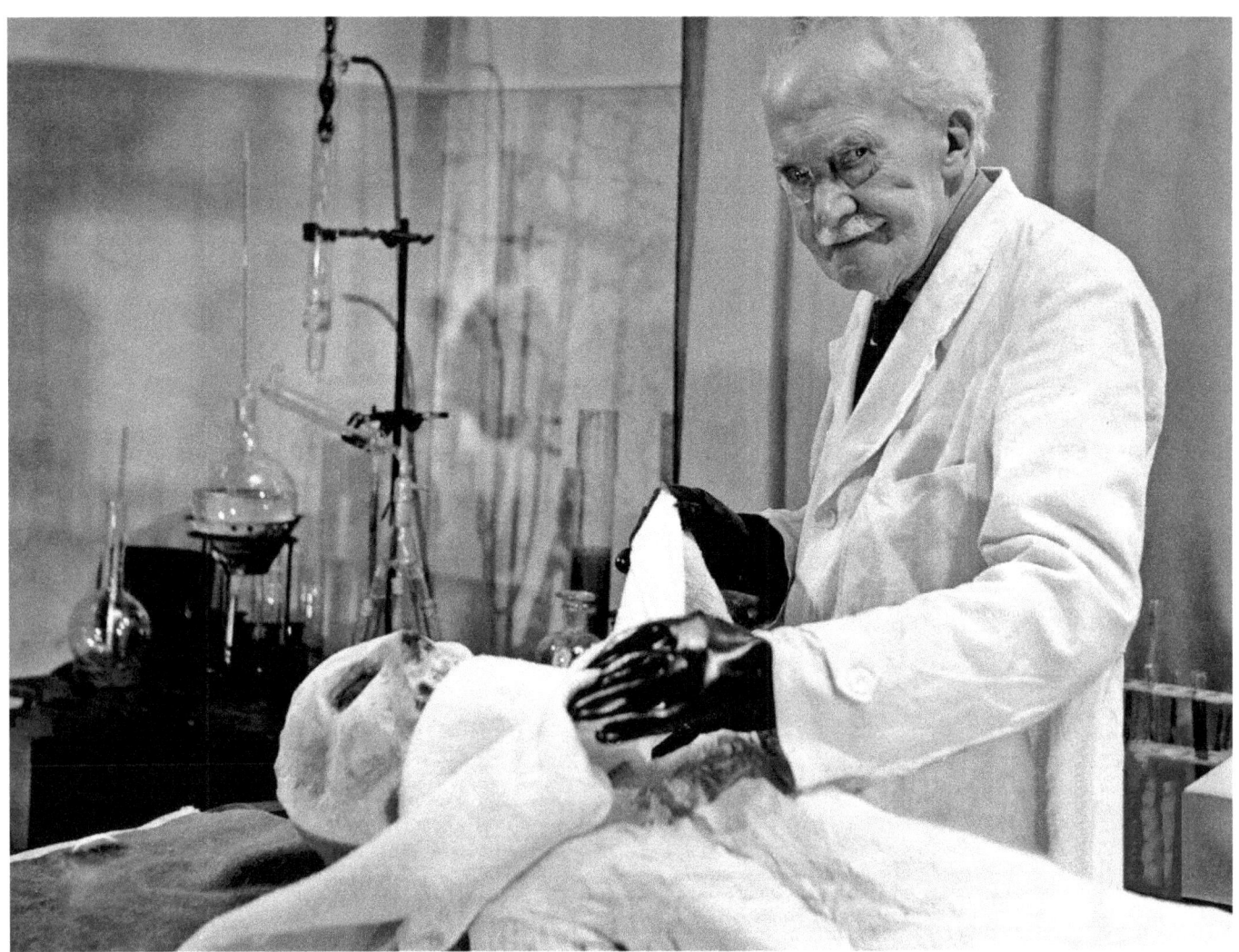

DIE NYLONSCHLINGE
("The Nylon Noose")
Production: Germany, 1963
Director: Rudolf Zehetgruber
Category: Krimi
A German *gruselkrimi* in the macabre vein of the popular Rialto/Edgar Wallace films of that period, concerning a killer who strangles his victims with nylon rope. With plenty of grotesque flourishes, plus scenes shot in a strip bar.

PARANOIAC

Production: UK, 1963

Director: Freddie Francis

Category: Maniac

Starting with **Taste Of Fear** in 1961, Hammer Films produced a string of sub-**Psycho** thrillers over the next few years. **Paranoiac** is one of the most enjoyable, featuring as it does an early performance from the great Oliver Reed and a host of cunning plot twists in telling the tale of Simon (Reed), a disturbed young man who we see playing an organ requiem in a chapel for the baby brother he has supposedly killed. Shocks, tentative gore effects and outré props add to the convincingly chilling atmosphere.

QUESTO MONDO PROIBITO
("This Forbidden World")
Production: Italy, 1963
Director: Fabrizio Gabella
Category: Mondo
A controversial mondo movie which focused on sado-masochism, including scenes of bondage, torture and crucifixion.

LA RAGAZZA CHE SAPEVA TROPPO
("The Girl Who Knew Too Much")
Production: Italy, 1963
Director: Mario Bava
English release tile: **The Evil Eye**
Category: Giallo

Said by some to be the film which laid the grounds for the modern *giallo* genre to take off, and it was the same director who cemented its rise with his seminal offering **Sei Donne Per L'Assassino** the following year. Other notable proto-*giallo* films from the same period would include **Delitto Allo Specchio, 24 Ore Di Terrore, La Jena Di Londra**, and **Crimine A Due** (all 1964).

THE SADIST
Production: USA, 1963
Director: James Landis
Category: Serial Killer

The first real cinematic approximation of the sensational case of teenage rockabilly killer Charles Starkweather and his jailbait moll, Caril Fugate. Starkweather, born 1940 in Lincoln, Nebraska, was a garbageman from a poor family, a teen rebel with a James Dean quiff who harboured a mess of rage and hatred in his soul. Fugate, who was 14 when they met, was also rebellious and the couple forged an intense white trash romance, much to her parents' displeasure. On December 1, 1957 Charlie – long brooding over plans of vengeance against the world – finally exploded, committing a violent robbery/murder at a gas station. On January 28, an argument broke out between Charlie and Caril's father, and the teenage assassin responded by killing her entire family. After spending some time alone in the house (they stashed the dead bodies in the barn), Starkweather and Fugate hit the road, leaving a trail of corpses in their dust. Their victims included an elderly couple and their maid, a family friend of the Starkweathers, and a young couple named Robert Jensen and Carole King; King's partially stripped body was tossed in a storm drain, viciously stabbed through the genitals and rectum. Finally, after a week of mayhem, the Nebraska police caught up with their victim, the ultimate juvenile delinquent, born bad and headed straight to Hell. Charlie Starkweather fried in the electric chair on June 24, 1959; Carole Fugate received a sentence of life imprisonment.

DER SCHWARZE ABT
("The Black Abbot")
Production: Germany, 1963
Director: Franz Josef Gottlieb
Category: Krimi

From the novel of the same name, this is among the more gothic entries in Rialto's 60s Edgar Wallace series of corpse-littered crime enigmas. An insane aristocrat falls victim to his shady butler (Klaus Kinski), and the hooded figure of a sinister monk appears as the body count starts to rise. Like many of these *gruselkrimis*, **Der Schwarze Abt** is more interesting for its uncanny imagery, and the lurid contortions of Kinski, than the actual plot, and bears much resemblence to the later entry **Der Unheimliche Mönch**.

SHOCK CORRIDOR

Production: USA, 1963
Director: Sam Fuller
Category: Insanity

Fuller, a former crime reporter, directed a series of tough pulp movies in various genres from 1949 onwards, including war films (**The Steel Helmet**, 1951) and westerns (**Forty Guns**, 1957), and winning acclaim for his kinetic noir thriller **Pick-Up On South Street** (1953). But it was with two films released in 1963 and 1964 respectively, **Shock Corridor** and **The Naked Kiss**, that Fuller achieved the paroxysmatic peak of his frequently violent and sordid cine-aesthetic. Set in an insane asylum, **Shock Corridor** details a murder investigation that ends in schizophrenia and mental collapse amongst an array of lunatics, sexual deviants and the walking damned.

TABETA HITO
("Eating People")
Production: Japan, 1963
Director: Kazufumi Fujino
Category: Cannibalism
Violent, surrealistic sensory assault as a waitress dreams that the chef is carving her open and extracting various objects, including a human eye. Her contents are then served to the hungry customers. When she wakes up, she vomits an interminable length of string that finally binds and meshes all the diners.

I TABÙ
("Taboos")
Production: Italy, 1963
Director: Romolo Marcellini
English release title: **Taboos Of The World**
Category: Mondo
Early "shock' mondo movie, with Vincent Price as narrator. Includes scenes of ritual finger amputation, and footage from inside a leper colony, as well as the usual weirdness and exotica. Marcellini followed up with **I Tabù No. 2** (also known as **Macabro**) in 1965.

DIE WEISSE SPINNE
("The White Spider")
Production: Germany, 1963
Director: Harald Reinl
Category: Krimi

A German *gruselkrimi* in the macabre vein of the popular Rialto/Edgar Wallace films of that period, with Rialto/Wallace regulars Joachim Fuchsberger and Karin Dor, plus director Harald Reinl (married to Dor at the time). The White Spider is an underground criminal network which ultimately turns out to be just one man, a master of disguise and deception. Director Reinl ended up like one of the victims in his films, stabbed to death in Spain by his second wife, in 1986.

WHEELS OF TRAGEDY
Production: USA, 1963
Director: Richard Wayman
Category: Driver Education/Auto-Carnage

28-minute driver educational film, the final part of Wayman's shocking gore trilogy produced by the Highway Safety Foundation. Bloody accident scenes with pulped corpses are counterpointed by reconstructions of the events which may have led up to their occurrence. A few years after this film came out, rumours started to circulate that the HSF was also involved in clandestine porn film production, and Wayman departed leaving his partner, Earle Deems, in charge of future auto-carnage productions such as **The Third Killer** (1966) and **Highways Of Agony** (1969).

DER WÜRGER VON SCHLOSS BLACKMOOR
("The Strangler Of Blackmoor Castle")
Production: Germany, 1963
Director: Harald Reinl
Category: Krimi

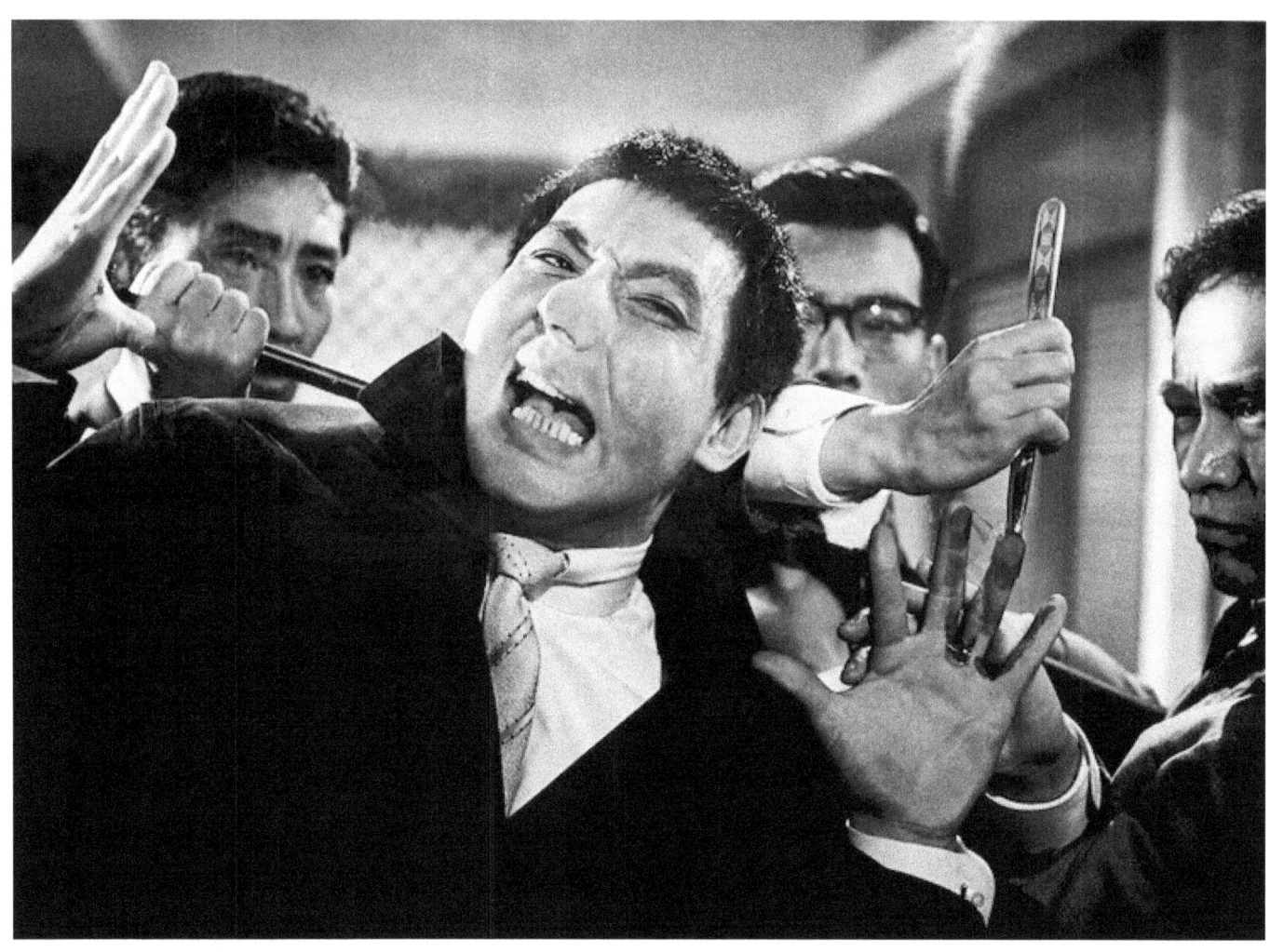

YAJU NO SEISHUN
("Youth Of The Wild Beast")
Production: Japan, 1963
Director: Seijun Suzuki
Category: Yazuka

Seijun Suzuki, latterly acclaimed as one of the greatest Japanese film directors of all time, was an innovator hamstrung by his contractual attachment to Nikkatsu, a commercial company bent on pumping out popular hit movies; their modus operandi can be gleaned just by the titilating titles of some of the films they made Suzuki direct near the start of his career: **Suppadeka No Nenrei** ("Age Of Nudity"), **Rajo To Kenju** ("Nude Girl With A Gun"), **Aoi Chibusa** ("Young Breasts"). But Suzuki really found his directorial voice with a series of *yakuza* films starting with **Yaju No Seishun**, a project where Suzuki unleashed his imagination to create a startling blend of brutal violence, black humour, nihilism and narrative ellipses, while still managing to work within Nikkatsu's stipulated parameters – just.

ZAPRUDER FILM: THE ASSASSINATION OF JOHN F. KENNEDY
Production: USA, 1963
Director: Abraham Zapruder
Category: Documentary/Death
This silent, 26-second 8mm "home movie" of US President John F Kennedy's motorcade moving through Dealey Plaza, Dallas on November 22 1963, ended up as the most complete and detailed footage of Kennedy's assassination. Zapruder's film is notable for clearly capturing the fatal head shot which blasted chunks of the President's skull and brain across the rear of his limousine, making it the most famous "snuff" movie in history. Debate remains over whether Zapruder's original footage was at some point doctored to remove certain evidence. The fatal head shot is also captured in less publicized films made by Orville Nix, Marie Muchmore, and Charles Bronson (not the actor). In 1998, the footage was digitally restored and enhanced to be included in the documentary **Image Of An Assassination**. Just two days after Kennedy was killed, his alleged assassin Lee Harvey Oswald was also gunned down in a Texas jailhouse, shot at point-blank range by nightclub owner Jack Ruby. This was also captured on motion film, and the footage can be seen in a Universal-International newsreel entitled **Assassin Killed**, with narration by Ed Herlihy. Ruby's strip joint, the Carousal, can be glimpsed in Larry Buchanan's sexploitation effort **Naughty Dallas**, released the following year, which told the story of a country girl who enters a burlesque dancing contest at the Colony Club in Dallas, wins, and becomes one of the city's leading strippers.

A PATY JEZDEC JE STRACH
("And The Fifth Horseman Is Fear")
Production: Czechoslovakia, 1964
Director: Zbynek Brynych
Category: Fascism
A meditation on fear that uses totalitarianism as its framework in a drama of struggle and betrayal. A doctor in Nazi-occupied Europe searching for illicit drugs is drawn into a netherworld of brothels with enslaved Jewish women as sex slaves and a lunatic asylum for Jews driven mad by persecution, all the while aware that informants are watching his every move.

AIMEZ-VOUS DES FEMMES?
("Do You Like Women?")
Production: France, 1964
Director: Jean Léon
Category: Cannibalism
Black comedy about a society of Japanese cannibals in Paris, who serve up tasty young girls for dinner on the full moon. The original scenario was devised by Roman Polanski, and Polanski's long-term collaborator Gerard Brach provides the dialogue.

THE BEAUTIFUL, THE BLOODY, AND THE BARE
Production: USA, 1964
Director: Sande N. Johnsen
Category: Psycho-Nudie
Nudie which adds an early element of the "psycho-slasher" genre. A fashion photographer in New York turns homicidal at the sight of the colour red, resulting in the slaughter of most of his models. Most of the film is shots of these models undressing, showering etc, and there's not much blood, but it stands as a primitive precursor to the scopophiliac sex-murder fusion of the later *giallo* genre.

BYLEM KAPO
("I Was A Kapo")
Production: Poland, 1964
Director: Tadeusz Jaworski
Category: Atrocity
The confessions of a former Nazi death camp captain, who rose through the ranks at Auschwitz. He recounts his crimes against humanity on camera, no longer a beast in uniform but an ordinary, middle-aged man. Survivors who knew him also add their testimony.

THE CHILD MOLESTER
Production: USA, 1964
Director: Herbert J. Leder
Category: Sex Crimes
Produced by the educational Highway Safety Foundation, who were notorious for their ultra-gory car-crash films, **The Child Molester** is a short cautionary film warning children about predatory paedophiles, and is equally hard-hitting. Actually based on the real-life case of Gerald Ray Howell, who abducted, raped and killed two young girls, the film dramatizes the events leading up to the girls' deaths, and then hammers home its message by showing actual crime scene footage of their corpses, with blood and brains splattered out from caved-in skulls. A truly horrific ending, in tune with the HSF's policy of unflinching depictions of the human carnage that can result from carelessness. (As it turned out, police interviews with the killer, Howell, led to revelations of intense homosexual activity in a local public bathroom; the police enlisted the help of the HSF to secretly film this activity through a two-way mirror; the resulting footage, titled simply **Camera Surveillance**, was subsequently used in police training.) Director Leder also made horror movies (such as **The Frozen Dead** and **It!**), but returned to child abuse for his final film, **The Candy Man** (1969), in which a sleazy drugs pusher in Mexico City singles out a film star's young daughter for kidnap.

GESTAPOMAN SCHMIDT
Production: Poland, 1964
Director: Jerzy Ziarnik
Category: Atrocity
Schmidt, an unknown Nazi bureaucrat, left behind his personal photograph album during the retreat from Warsaw. It contained 380 photos, mostly of beatings, torture, and executions carried out by himself and his accomplices in the Gestapo. Ziarnik's documentary presents a horrifying selection of these images, captioned only by the name of each victim.

LA GRANDE FROUSSE
("The Big Fright")
Production: France, 1964
Director: Jean-Pierre Mocky
Category: Atrocity
One of only two features to be based on the novels of Jean Ray (the other being Harry Kumel's **Malpertuis**), **La Grande Frousse** is based on Ray's *La Cité de*

l'Indicible Peur, written in 1943. When a forger escapes from the guillotine, a police inspector tracks him down to the provincial town of Barges, a weird community whose residents all live in fear of a sinister, predatory beast which apparently roams the surrounding countryside. An alcoholic doctor, a love-sick butcher, and other absurd figures add to Mocky's anarchic concoction, which mixes elements of farce and the grotesque. Sadly, for its initial release in 1964, the film suffered from poor editing at the hands of its distributors, who tipped it towards slapstick. When the rights reverted to Jean-Pierre Mocky in 1973, he reconstructed the film as he had originally intended it, reinserting some cut sequences, giving it the title of the novel on which it was based, and tilting its equilibrium back to the nightside.

HYSTERIA
Production: UK, 1964
Director: Freddie Francis
Category: Psychosis
Hysteria was the last, and most complex, of five "psycho-thriller" movies produced by Hammer Films between 1960 and 1964 (the others being **Taste Of Fear**, **Paranoiac**, **Maniac**, and **Nightmare**), the story of an American accident victim with amnesia in London. Warned by his doctor to expect hallucinations, he is given the use of a flat and soon begins to see some horrifying visions...

KALEIDOSCOPE
Production: UK, 1964-67
Director: Alfred Hitchcock
Category: Maniac

Hitchcock's aborted, experimental serial rapist/killer film, which he intended to be a radical change in his style. Using gruesome details from the true-life UK murder case of Neville Heath (although the script featured a necrophiliac killer in New York), the director constructed a framework over which he intended to employ such devices as hand-held cameras and natural light, the action all seen from the murderer's perspective. But censors quashed his plans, claiming the protagonist was too "ugly", the subject matter too dark. All that remains is an hour of silent test footage, plus a few pre-production stills illustrating the film's intended "terror highlights" (including a murder at a waterfall). Some of Hitchcock's ideas for **Kaleidoscope** would later be recycled in his sleazy 1972 film **Frenzy**. Neville Heath committed at least two sex-murders in 1946; both female victims had been stripped nude, bound and tortured, with nipples bitten off and violent vaginal trauma caused by rape with a sharp object.

KAWAITA HANA
("Dead Flowers")
Production: Japan, 1964
Director: Masahiro Shinoda
Category: Yakuza

Muraki, a *yakuza* hit-man, is released from prison and becomes obsessed with Saeko, a mysterious young woman involved in the underworld of gambling and drug addiction. Inevitably, Muraki ends up killing a rival gang member and returning to jail; he later learns that Saeko has been murdered by a drug addict. Director Shinoda charts this doomed relationship with stylistic innovations that place his film in the avant-garde of early 1960s crime cinema; complaints from the screenwriter that his dialogue was lost in this "anarchic" approach actually delayed release for several months. **Kawaita Hana** is known by the English release title **Pale Flower**.

THE KILLERS
Production: USA, 1964
Director: Don Siegel
Category: Post-Noir/Crime
One of the few essential post-noir, shot-in-colour American crime films. Director Siegel would later make another, **Dirty Harry**, while Lee Marvin would appear in two more, **Point Blank** and **Prime Cut**.

KITTEN WITH A WHIP
Production: USA, 1964
Director: Douglas Heyes
Category: Crime

KWAHERI: VANISHING AFRICA
Production: USA, 1964
Director: Thor Brooks, David Chudnow
Category: Mondo
Officially directed by "Mr & Mrs Nikki Carter", this mondo documentary in the tradition of **Karamoja** features all the usual African atrocities and more, including giant-cocked pygmy sex orgies, witch doctors, facial disfigurements, giant snake attacks, open-brain surgery, and drug-driven sex rituals in which a virgin is supposedly burnt alive.

MOB AND RIOT CONTROL
Production: USA, 1964
Category: Police Violence
Film produced for police only (in English and Spanish versions) by the Charles Cahill Company, dealing with law enforcement procedures in the control of civil disobedience. This is the seminal police brutality moving-picture manual that would

equip US riot squads with all the techniques they needed to suppress the various demonstrations of the 60s – tear-gassing, smashing with batons, and quasi-military battle formations.

MONDO BALORDO
Production: Italy, 1964
Director: Roberto Bianchi Montero
Category: Mondo
Weird mondo from Montero, narrated by horror icon Boris Karloff. The film's sequences include a transvestite lesbian nightclub, a dwarf rock singer, Asian brothels and bondage, duelling German students, a dwarf/normal love affair, and Arab women dying their hair blond using camel urine. There's also the usual amount of animal cruelty, with live prey shown being torn apart and devoured by native hunters.

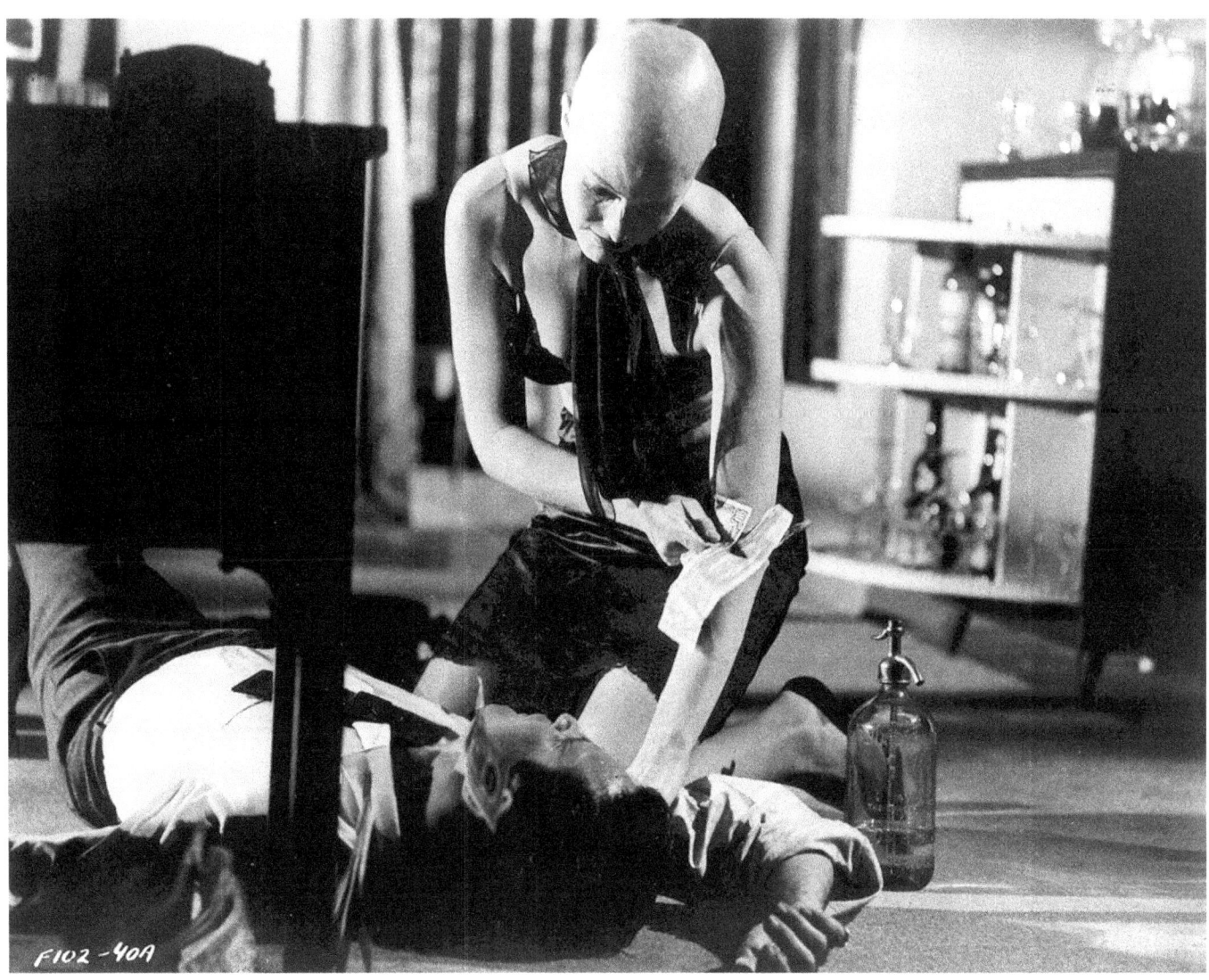

THE NAKED KISS
Production: USA, 1964
Director: Sam Fuller
Category: Pulp Noir

NIGHTMARE
Production: UK, 1964
Director: Freddie Francis
Category: Psychosis

Another well-made, Jimmy Sangster-scripted Hammer psycho movie concerning a young girl (Jennie Linden) who sees apparitions of a white-shrouded figure which eventually lead her to a bloody corpse. The basic premise recalled Hammer's earlier **Taste Of Fear**, and added little new to the post-**Diaboliques** sub-genre save for some intriguing cinematography and camera-shots from director Francis, which lend the necessary edge of dark oneirism.

DAS PHANTOM VON SOHO
("The Phantom Of Soho")
Production: Germany, 1964
Director: Franz Josef Gottlieb
Category: Krimi

RED ASPHALT
Production: USA, 1964
Category: Driver Education/Auto-Carnage
One of the pioneering films in the educational "driver safety" sub-genre, presented by the California Highway Patrol. **Red Asphalt** was a grim warning against the dangers of speed on the highway, featuring graphic scenes of real-life car-wrecks and mangled corpses, complete with human entrails being scooped off the road and into plastic bags. This is absolute horror at its most unforgiving, with no dressing-up, starker and more sickening than any mondo movie. The film is periodically updated and new scenes cut in, to maintain its relevance to young drivers of the day; **Red Asphalt 4** came out in 1998, with production values and techniques vastly evolved from the original.

SEI DONNE PER L'ASSASSINO
("Six Women For the Killer")
Production: Italy, 1964
Director: Mario Bava
US title: **Blood And Black Lace**
Category: Giallo

SHADES AND DRUMBEATS
Production: USA, 1964
Director: Andrew Meyer
Category: Beat Culture
A 25-minute silent colour record of an all-night party where young hipsters freely indulge in sex and drugs, this a little-known Beat classic to sit beside others like Larry Moyer's **The Moving Finger** or Harold Lea's beat-slasher hybrid **The Fat Black Pussycat**, both released a year earlier.

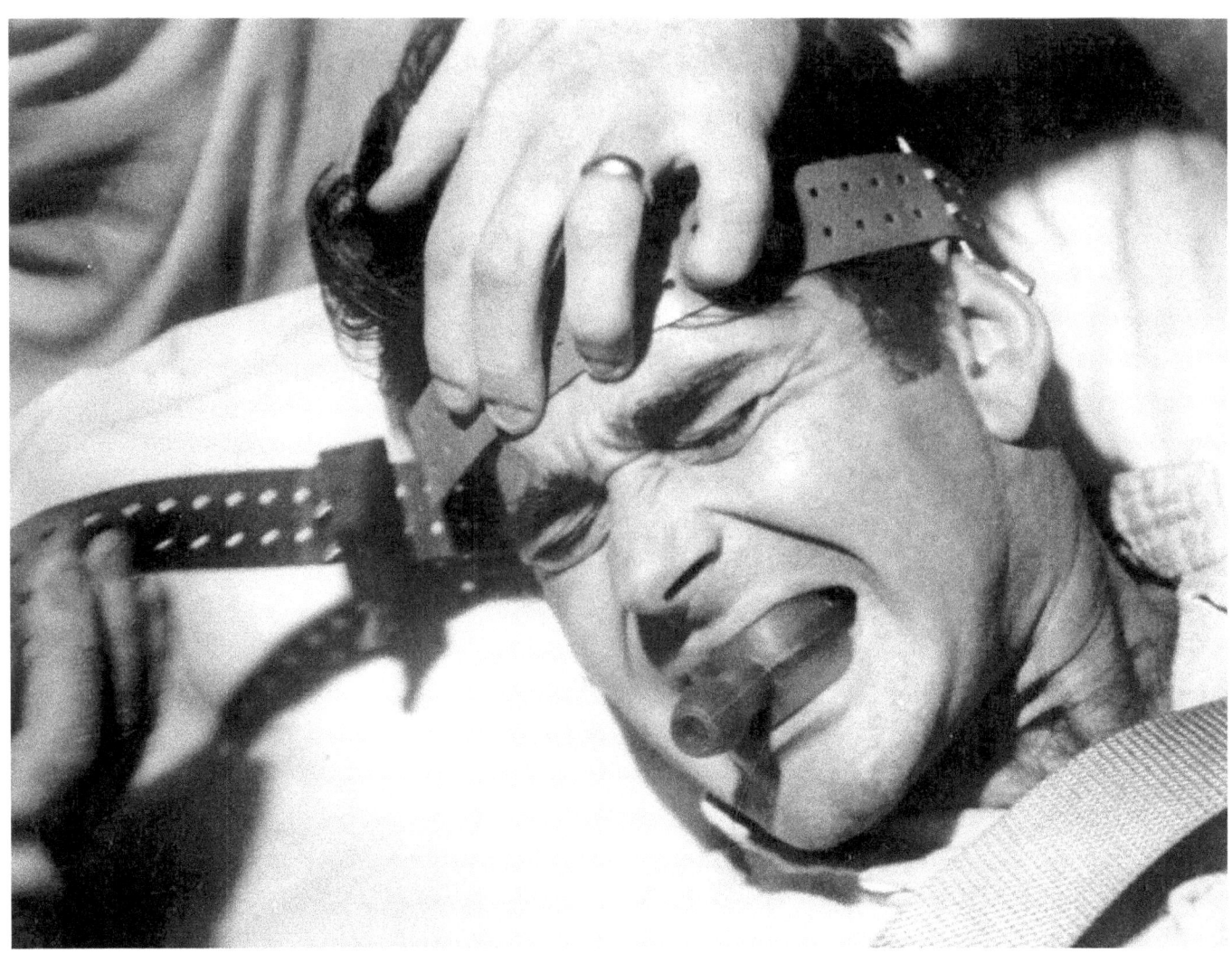

SHOCK TREATMENT
Production: USA, 1964
Director: Denis Sanders
Category: Crime/Insanity
This post-noir dive into the world of evil examines how money retains the power to drive people to (literally) lose their minds, whilst exposing the unfettered cruelty in mental institutions often meted out by corrupt administrators. Gruelling electro-therapy scenes combine with an obsessive search for stolen money which, when found to have been reduced to ashes, snaps the sanity of the asylum's unscrupulous doctor.

STRAITJACKET
Production: USA, 1964
Director: William Castle
Category: Maniac

THE STRANGLER
Production: USA, 1964
Director: Burt Topper
Category: Maniac
Inspired by the Boston Strangler, still an unsolved case at time of production.

THE THRILL KILLERS
Production: USA, 1964
Director: Ray Dennis Steckler
Category: Maniac
Steckler's psycho-killer movie follows several escaped lunatics and killers who embark on a savage murder spree across Los Angeles. With stripper Liz Renay, who also appeared in the 1965 maniac movie **Day Of The Nightmare**.

THE TRIAL OF LEE HARVEY OSWALD
Production: USA, 1964
Director: Larry Buchanan
Category: True Crime
One of the weirdest true crime movies ever; using a cast of amateur actors, Buchanan creates for the cinema a posthumous trial of Lee Harvey Oswald, the man accused of assasinating John F. Kennedy; Oswald was actually gunned down by Jack Ruby, a Dallas strip-bar owner, before his case could be heard. Unfortunately, the result is very boring. A disclaimer stating the film was suppressed immediately after its first showing due to "unwarranted pressures" adds an edge of conspiracy theory that would blossom in Buchanan's later **Down On Us** (1984), which speculates that the CIA murdered counter-culture icons Jim Morrison, Janis Joplin and Jimi Hendrix.

TWO ON A GUILLOTINE
Production: USA, 1964
Director: William Conrad
Category: Psycho Thriller
An attempt to emulate William Castle's brand of horror-tinged suspense/mystery films, involving a supposedly haunted house and a fake beheading. Released in 1965, as was Conrad's next film **Brainstorm**, concerning a killer who fakes insanity to escape jail, but then is truly driven mad during his incarceration at the local lunatic asylum.

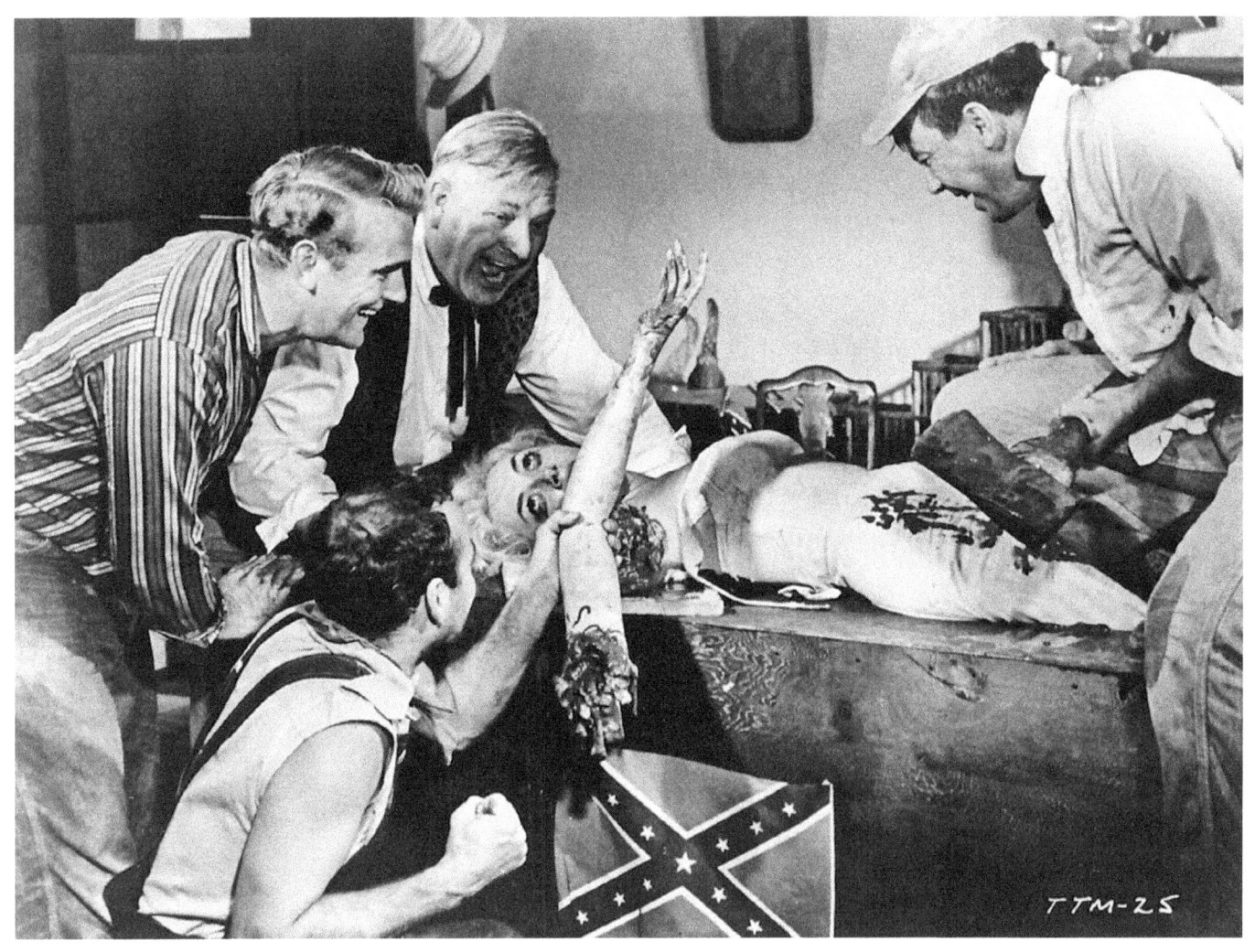

TWO THOUSAND MANIACS
Production: USA, 1964
Director: Hercshell Gordon Lewis
Category: Psychosis/Gore

For his second gore movie, Lewis created a scenario where six strangers are lured to a southern town and then butchered one by one as revenge for cimes committed during the Civil War. His other film of 1964, **Moonshine Mountain,** pursued a different white trash theme, this time concentrating more on the criminal manufacture and distribution of illicit liquor than gore.

DAS UNGEHEUER VON LONDON CITY

("The Monster Of London City")
Production: Germany, 1964
Director: Edwin Zbonek
Category: Krimi

Perhaps the most lurid of the 60s *grüselkrimi* films produced by CCC in collaboration with Bryan Edgar Wallace, **Das Ungeheuer Von London City** concerns a spate of Jack the Ripper-style murders in London, which take place at the same time as a new stage-play about the Ripper starts production. The usual compelling pulp visual style is here allied to a gruesome murder thematic and even flashing glimpses of female nudity. Although no further CCC/Wallace films were released for the next seven years, exploitation master Jesus Franco finally stepped in with two German/Spanish productions: **Der Teufel Kam Aus Akasava** (actually based on the Edgar Wallace story "The Akasava"), ramping up the sex and violence to 70s levels. A German/Italian production, Armando Crispino's **L'Etrusco Uccide Ancora** (1972, based on another Bryan Edgar Wallace short story) swiftly followed, but that was the end for CCC. Franco also directed a Copercines production, **Der Todesrächer Von Soho,** based on the Bryan Edgar Wallace story "Death Packs A Suitcase".

UNTITLED [THE HANGING FILMS OF ANATOLY SLIVKO]

Production: Russia, 1964-85
Director: Anatoly Slivko
Category: Snuff Film

Anatoly Slivko was arrested in December 1985, and accused of seven murders, sexual violation and necrophilia. Since 1964, Slivko had abused his position as a children's club leader to indulge in fetishistic sexual fantasies which involved the simulated hanging of young boys between the ages of 13 and 17; Slivko would induce unconsciousness by controlled hanging, and then molest his victims and masturbate. He also filmed and photographed each "experiment". When one boy accidentally died, Slivko was set on path of murder; at least seven boys in total were hanged until dead, raped, dismembered, and set on fire while Slivko ejaculated over their burning corpses. He was finally found out and arrested after 21 years, and executed by gunshot in 1989. The 8mm films which survived him, showing his young victims hanging until unconscious and, in many cases, dead, are amongst the most harrowing and twisted of that rarefied species, the serial killer home movie. It remains unclear whether they have all been destroyed by Russian authorities, or whether some remain under lock and key.

MACISTE CONTRO I MONGOLI
("Maciste Vs. The Mongols")
Production: Italy, 1963
Director: Domenico Paolella
English release title: **Hercules Against The Mongols**
Category: Peplum

MYTH

I DIECI GLADIATORI
("The Ten Gladiators")
Production: Italy, 1963
Director: Gianfranco Parolini
Category: Peplum

A FINNISH FABLE
Production: USA, 1963
Director: Carmen D'Avino
Category: Fantasy
A quietly disturbing animated fantasy played out by grotesque, naked male and female mannequins in various states of disrepair, including one with a severed head that moves around of its own accord. Like a Hans Bellmer wet-dream come to life, body parts become interchangeable and decorated in psychedelic motifs or cryptograms, the nude mannequins comport in various provocative visual compositions, and there is even a creepy "little girl" figure dancing in the woods. The film ends with one of the females being carried off by the director, followed by

the enigmatic, scrawled coda "time for crayfish". D'Avino made his first film, **Sunday Afternoon**, in 1951, winning a Creative Film Award (presented to him by Salvador Dali). He went on to make a series of acclaimed animations, including **Theme And Transition** (1956), **The Big O** (1958), **A Trip** (1960), and **Pianissimo** (1963, inspired by the pop record by legendary British comedian Ken Dodd).

JASON AND THE ARGONAUTS
Production: UK/USA, 1963
Director: Don Chaffey
Category: Myth

LABIRYNT
("Labyrinth")
Production: Poland, 1963
Director: Jan Lenica
Category: Fantasy/Animation

15-minute collage animation by former poster designer Lenica, whose earlier **Dom** (made in collaboration with Walerian Borowczyk) remains one of the best of all animated films from Eastern Europe. **Labirynt,** which garnered the director much international acclaim, is a surrealistic fable featuring a fugitive Icarus-figure seen gliding through classical cityscapes haunted by strange hybrid creatures and agents of control. Lenica's next film, the absurdist **Rhinoceros**, was made in what was then known as West Germany.

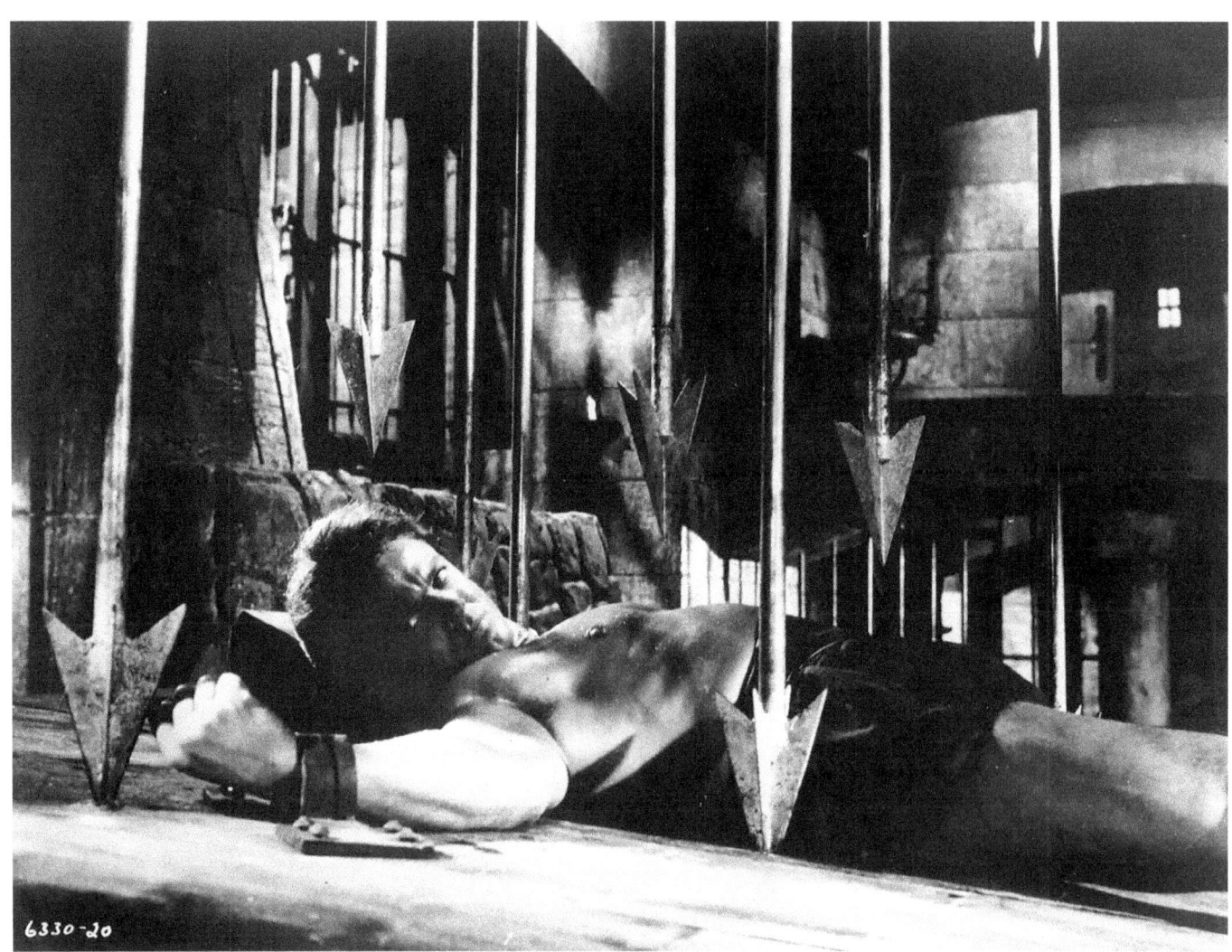

MACISTE L'EROE PIÙ GRANDE DEL MONDO
("Maciste, The World's Greatest Hero")
Production: Italy, 1963
Director: Michele Lupo
US release title: **Goliath And The Sins Of Babylon**
Category: Peplum

NEMURI KYOSHIRO SAPPOCHO
("Kyoshiro Nemuri: Murder Chronicles")
Production: Japan, 1963
Director: Tokuzo Tanaka
English release title: **Sleepy Eyes Of Death: The Chinese Jade**
Category: Chambara

Christianity was first brought to Japan by visiting Portuguese during the 1540s. After 1549, the Shogunate ordered the destruction of all churches and the deportation of all missionaries. Christians were persecuted on a mass scale, being crucified, beheaded, boiled in oil or burnt at the stake if they would not renounce their beliefs. In 1637, on the island of Amakusa, the Shoguns infamously harvested and buried 1,111 heads of Christians in their greatest-ever purge. This torture holocaust – depicted in such films as **Tokugawa Onna keibatsu-emaki: Ushi-zaki no kei** – forms the background for the character of Kyoshiro Nemuri, a roaming half-blood swordsman conceived during satanic rituals, who deals death with the "full moon cut" in a series of works which grew progressively more violent, erotic and nihilistic during the 1960s. Raizo Ichikawa stars as Nemuri, starting with **Nemuri Kyoshiro Sappocho** and ending some eleven episodes later with **Nemuri Kyoshiro Akujo-gari** (1969). Directors on the series included Kazuo Ikehiro and Kenji Misumi, who both went on to produce classic early 70s *chambara* hits. Nemuri was played by Hiroki Matsukata in two final 1969 episodes, but Raizo Ichikawa (who died in 1969 aged only 37) will always be remembered as the definitive Kyoshiro.

YUKINOJO HENGE
("Yukinojo's Strange Transformation")
Production: Japan, 1963
Director: Kon Ichikawa
English release title: **An Actor's Revenge**
Category: Chambara

Female roles in Japanese *kabuki* theatre are traditionally played by male actors, known as *onnagata*, or *oyama*. This duality is perhaps best explored cinematically in Ichikawa's **Yukinojo Henge**, in which the eponymous female impersonator avenges the death of his parents by a complicated scheme of duplicities which function on many levels of opposition. The film's visual complexity is equally ingenious, as Ichikawa utilises notions of *kabuki* to manipulate screen-space, perspective, lighting and characterisation. The tradition of cross-dressing was also typified by transvestite lead actors Maruyama Akihiro in the ultra-camp **Kurotokage** (1968), and Peter in Toshio Matsumoto's experimental **Bara No Soretsu** (1969).

BAKUMATSU ZANKOKU MONOGATARI
("Cruel Story From The Bakamatsu Period")
Production: Japan, 1964
Director: Tai Kato
Category: Chambara

As its title suggests, this is one of the bloodiest and most perverse *chambara* films of the 1960s, set one hundred years earlier in the 1860s just before the fall of the Shogun. At that time a band of rebel samurai rose up, known as the *Shinsen-gumi*; fiercely loyal to the Shogun, they stopped at nothing to achieve their aim of derailing the Meiji Restoration. Unlike some previous films on the subject, director Kato does nothing to dilute historical accuracy in his depiction of the *Shinsen-gumi* – they are shown as a filthy, murderous, half-insane group of fanatics whose legendary cruelty is also unflinchingly dealt with. If any man tried to leave their organsiation, he would be summarily executed – slashed with swords and left to bleed to death, or else brutally decapitated. Their leader was originally Serizawa Kamo, but he was assasinated and succeeded by Kondo Isami, aided by his sadistic, homosexual enforcer, Hijikata Toshizo. In **Bakumatsu zankoku monogatari,** Serizawa's nephew infiltrates the group with the intent to murder Kondo. The *Shinsen-gumi* ended as military force with the beheading of Kondo Isami on May 17, 1868, and the killing in battle of Hijikata Toshizo on June 20, 1869. Kato next made the film many consider his masterpiece, the period *yakuza* explosion **Meiji kyokyakuden sandaime shumei.**

DEUS E O DIABO NA TERRA DO SOL
("God And The Devil In The Land Of The Sun")
Production: Brazil, 1964
Director: Glauber Rocha
Category: Historical

Regarded as a key work in early *Cinema Novo*, the new wave of Brazilian cinema which erupted in the 1960s with Rocha as its figurehead. Most films in this period of the movement tended to focus on north-eastern economic misery and mythology, the *favela*'s daily struggles, and a revolutionary historical revisionism. **Deus E O Diabo Na Terra Do Sol** falls into this latter category (as do others such as Nelson Pereira dos Santos' **Vidas Secas** (1963), Ruy Guerra's **Os Fuzis** (1963), and Carlos Diegues' **Ganga Zumba** (1964). Rocha's film, known in English as **Black God, White Devil**, features an assassin, Antônio das Mortes, who would return in an eponymous sequel in 1969.

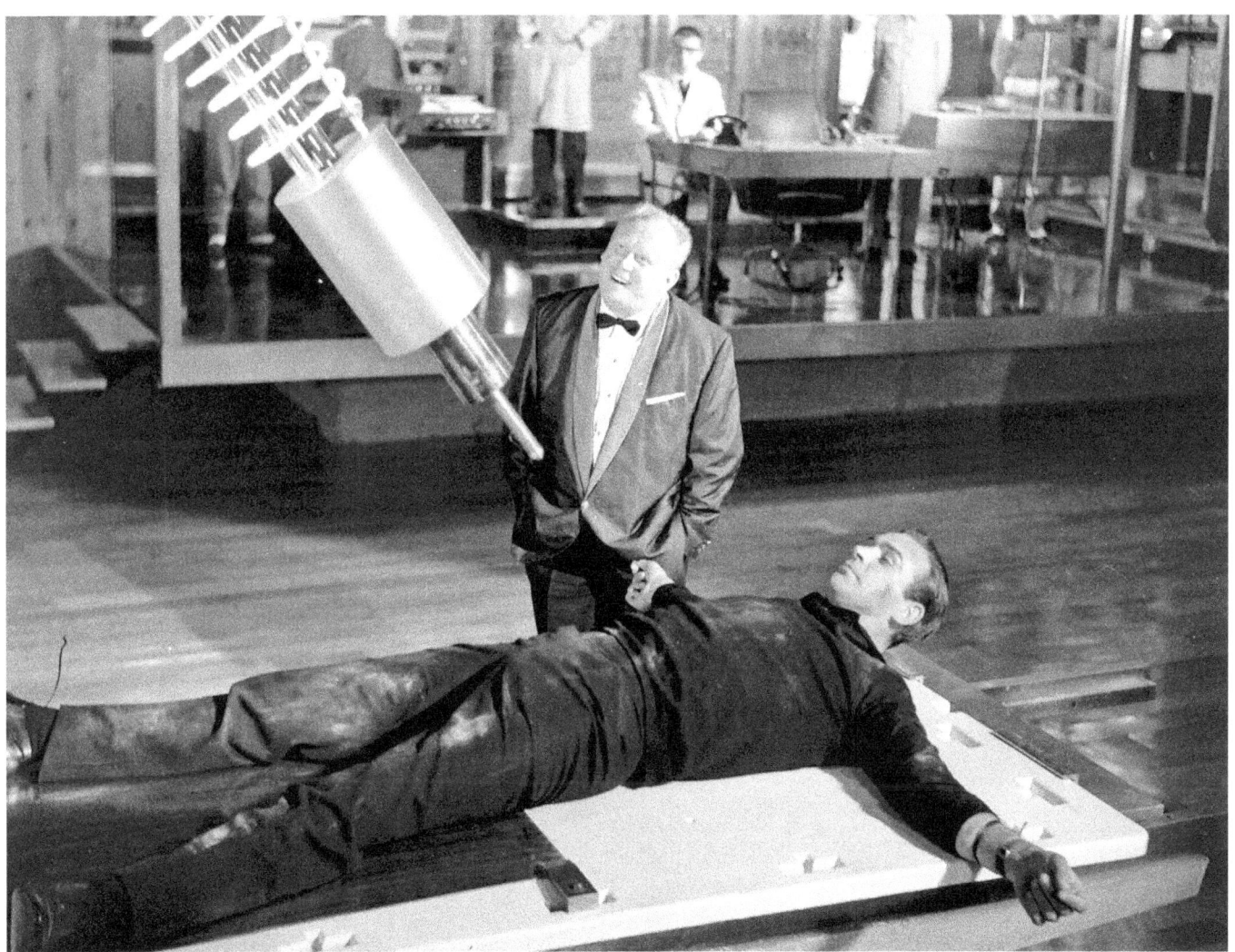

GOLDFINGER
Production: UK, 1964
Director: Guy Hamilton
Category: Super-Spy

The release of the third James Bond movie – maybe the best of them all – firmly established a new cinematic icon for the 20th century, creating the mythos of the super-spy. **Goldfinger** is the film in which a (nearly) naked Shirley Eaton is gold-painted to death and Bond is almost emasculated by a laser beam; it also features Bond's first rocket-launching car (an Aston Martin DB5), a girl gang of high-flyers led by lesbian Pussy Galore (Honor Blackman), the homicidal Japanese hat-throwing henchman Oddjob, and German Gert Frobe in the title role as the quintessential megalomaniac villain. This was the blueprint for a global craze of camp, gadget- and girl-infested spy/crime sagas, ranging from the Ian Fleming-sanctioned US TV show **The Man From U.N.C.L.E.** (1964-67, 105 episodes) to a whole "Eurospy" sub-genre, mostly consisting of low-budget Italian productions or co-productions. Shirley Eaton turned up again in Lindsay Shonteff's **Million Eyes Of Sumuru** (UK, 1967), produced by Harry Alan Towers, but the biggest-budget Bond pastiche of them – **Se Tutte Le Donne Del Mondo** (1966), produced by Dino De Laurentiis and directed by Henry Levin with Arduino Maiuri – was Italian, and an Italian actress, Monica Vitti, was chosen to play the title-role in **Modesty Blaise** (UK, 1966), the adventures of a "female James Bond". Ian Fleming's first Bond novel was 1953's *Casino Royale*; the first Bond movie was **Dr. No**, in 1962, followed by **From Russia With Love** (1963). After **Goldfinger**, Sean Connery reprised the role of Bond in **Thunderball** (1965), **You Only Live Twice** (1967), and **Diamonds Are Forever** (1970), before sensibly quitting.

GLI INVINCIBILI DIECI GLADIATORI
("Ten Invincible Gladiators")
Production: Italy, 1964
Director: Nick Nostro
Category: Peplum

KUNOICHI NINPO
("Female Ninja Power")
Production: Japan, 1964
Director: Sadao Nakajima
Category: Ninja/Chambara

The introduction of a new sub-genre of *chambara*, featuring female *ninja* warriors who use erotic tricks to fight their enemies; a combination of martial arts, sex and the superhuman skills that would persist right through to the 1990s and the **Kunoichi Ninpo-cho** series, with numerous sex films set in feudal times appearing in between. **Kunoichi Ninpo** was followed by the same director's **Kunoichi Kesho** (also 1964) and **Ninpo Chushingura** (1965), directed by Yasuto Hasegawa.

MACISTE E LA REGINA DI SAMAR
("Maciste And The Queen Of Samar")
Production: Italy, 1964
Director: Giacomo Gentilomo
US release title: **Hercules Against The Moon Men**
Category: Peplum

PER UN PUGNO DI DOLLARI
("For A Fistful Of Dollars")
Production: Italy/Spain/Germany, 1964
Director: Sergio Leone
Category: Western

Stylised remake of Akira Kurosawa's **Yojimbo** that established the so-called "spaghetti western" genre – hinted at the previous year by Sergio Corbucci's **Massacro Al Grande Canyon** – and made a star of its leading actor, Clint Eastwood. Ennio Morricone, who created the film's distinctive score, also achieved instant recognition beyond his native country. Unlike **The Magnificent Seven**, Hollywood's moronic cowboy copy of Kurosawa's **Shichinin no Samurai**, Leone invests the material with stylistic originality and a cold brutality, setting the stage for countless films to come. The same production company also filmed Mario Caino's **Le Pistole Non Discutono** ("Pistols Don't Argue") around the same time, and another 1964 effort was **Per Un Dollar A Tucson Si Muore** ("For A Dollar In Tucson, You Die"), directed by Cesare Canevari and released in 1965.

LA RIVOLTA DEI SETTE
("Revolt Of The Seven")
Production: Italy, 1964
Director: Alberto De Martino
US release title: **Gladiators Seven**
Category: Peplum

ROMA CONTRO ROMA
("Rome vs. Rome")
Production: Italy, 1964
Director: Giuseppe Vari
Category: Peplum

The "horror-peplum" sub-genre reached its limits with this shadowy tale of undead soldiers, an evil sorcerer, deformed minions, intimations of rape, and plentiful swordplay. Known in the US as **War Of The Zombies**, it may now be pronounced as the first Italian zombie movie. Director Vari went on to shoot several intriguing westerns, including **Un Buco In Fronte** (shot in the Salone catacombs outside Rome) and **Prega Il Morto E Ammazza Il Vivo**, which starred Klaus Kinski in an enigmatic slow-burn of simmering malevolence.

GLI SCHIAVI PIÙ FORTI DEL MONDO
("The Strongest Slaves In The World")
Production: Italy, 1964
Director: Michele Lupo
US release title: **Revenge Of The Gladiators**
Category: Peplum

7 FACES OF DR. LAO
Production: USA, 1964
Director: George Pal
Category: Fantasy

LE TIGRE AIME LA CHAIR FRAÎCHE
("The Tiger Loves Fresh Flesh")
Production: France, 1964
Director: Claude Chabrol
Englih release title: **Code Name: Tiger**
Category: Eurospy
One of the first sub-Bond spy films, an attempt to establish the Tiger (played by Roger Hanin) as a secret agent to rival the original. One sequel did appear the following year, entitled **Le Tigre Se Parfume À La Dynamite** ("The Tiger Wears Dynamite For Perfume", released in English as **Our Agent Tiger**).

ZATOICHI SESSHO TABI
("Zatoichi: Death Trip")
Production: Japan, 1964
Director: Kenji Misumi
Category: Chambara
The eighth Zatoichi film, notable for being the second one directed by Misumi, one of the most dynamic and visceral film-makers in the *chambara* genre. **Zatoichi Sessho Tabi** actually anticipates Misumi's later **Kozure Okami** films with its narrative of the blind swordsman caring for an orphaned baby whilst fighting off a band of brutal assassins.

THE DAY OF THE TRIFFIDS
Production: UK, 1963
Director: Steve Sekely
Category: Science Fiction/Horror

SCI-FI

DOCTOR WHO

Production: UK, 1963
Director: Various
Category: Science Fiction

The seminal British science fiction television show, best remembered for its opening three seasons (1963 to 1966) which featured the original actor, William Hartnell, as the eponymous time-traveller. **Dr. Who** also boasted one of the earliest examples of electronic pop music in its theme music. Outstanding storylines from these series include the Daleks, a society of robots bent on exterminating humanity; the Cybermen, a race of malevolent cyborgs; and the Zarbi and Menoptra, giant insectile dwellers of Vortis, the Web Planet.

IKARIE XB1

Production: Czechoslovakia, 1963
Director: Jindrich Polák
Category: Science Fiction

Another rare SF film from the Eastern Bloc, shot in monochrome with superb interior sets and costumes, documenting a long space trip to a distant star, and the psychological effects on the cosmonauts. Along the way they encounter the debris of a United Nations ghost craft, as well as vaguely menacing computer malfunctions. A butchered and overdubbed version was released in the USA in 1964, titled **Voyage To The End Of The Universe**.

KAITEI GUNKAN
("Undersea Battleship")
Production: Japan, 1963
Director: Ishiro Honda
US release title: **Atragon**
Category: Science Fiction

THE MADMEN OF MANDORAS
Production: USA, 1963
Director: David Bradley
Category: Science Fiction

A group of Nazi survivors are hiding in South America with Adolf Hitler's head kept alive in a jar. Brilliant concept, terrible movie. One of several science fictional horror films of the period that featured Nazis and scientific experiments, such as **She Demons, The Flesh Eaters,** and **The Frozen Dead**. Filmed in 1962 and originally little more than an hour long, **The Madmen Of Mandoras** was extended by adding newly-shot footage in 1968, and sold to TV under the new title **They Saved Hitler's Brain**.

MATANGO
Production: Japan, 1963
Director: Ishiro Honda
Category: Science Fiction

THE SLIME PEOPLE
Production: USA, 1963
Director: Robert Hutton
Category: Science Fiction

TOWERS OPEN FIRE
Production: UK, 1963
Director: Antony Balch
Category: Science Fiction

The first experimental film collaboration between Balch and writer William S. Burroughs, with input from Brion Gysin and Ian Sommerville, is seemingly inspired by the section "Towers Open Fire' from Burroughs' key SF/cut-up novel, *Nova Express*. Running at around 12 minutes, the film consists of various sequences featuring Burroughs, including an attack on a sinister boardroom, as well as self-filmed shots of Balch masturbating, stock news footage, dream machine images, and shots of Paris. The narration by Burroughs is initially taken from his novel *The Soft Machine*, and ends with the spoken command "towers open fire!".

UNEARTHLY STRANGER
Production: UK, 1963
Director: John Krish
Category: Science Fiction

X

Production: USA, 1963
Director: Roger Corman
Alternative title: **X: The Man With The X-Ray Eyes**
Category: Science Fiction/Horror

A pulp masterpiece from Corman, in which Ray Milland plays a scientist who administers a wonder-drug to his eyes, resulting in "X-ray" vision – he can see through surfaces to the matter within. At first this gift is a boon, but things go wrong with an accidental death and he ends up as a fugitive mind-reader in a carnival, daily increasing his drug dosage. As his visionary powers increase, he finds he can see to the infinite core of time and space, a maddening delirium beautifully rendered by Corman. The film ends with a Biblical mutilation as the deranged Milland screams: "If thine eye offend thee, pluck it out!". Corman's pinnacle achievement. in the science fiction genre. In a similar vein was H.G. Lewis' unfinished An Eye For An Eye (1967).

CHILDREN OF THE DAMNED
Production: UK, 1964
Director: Anton M. Leader
Category: Science Fiction

THE EARTH DIES SCREAMING
Production: UK, 1964
Director: Terence Fisher
Category: Science Fiction
Fisher takes a break from Hammer to direct this 60-minute, monochrome alien invasion movie, in which humans are turned into eyeless zombies.

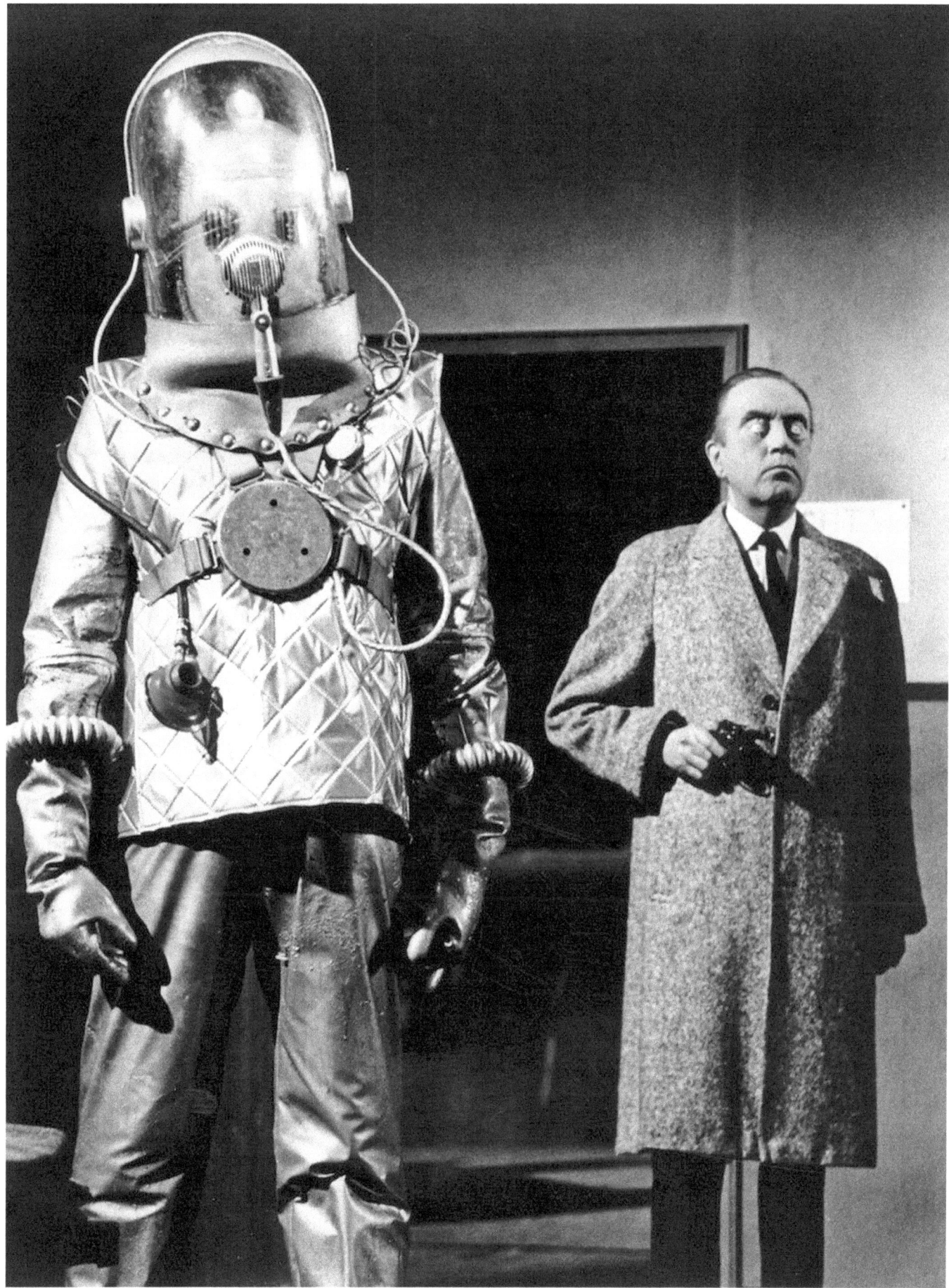

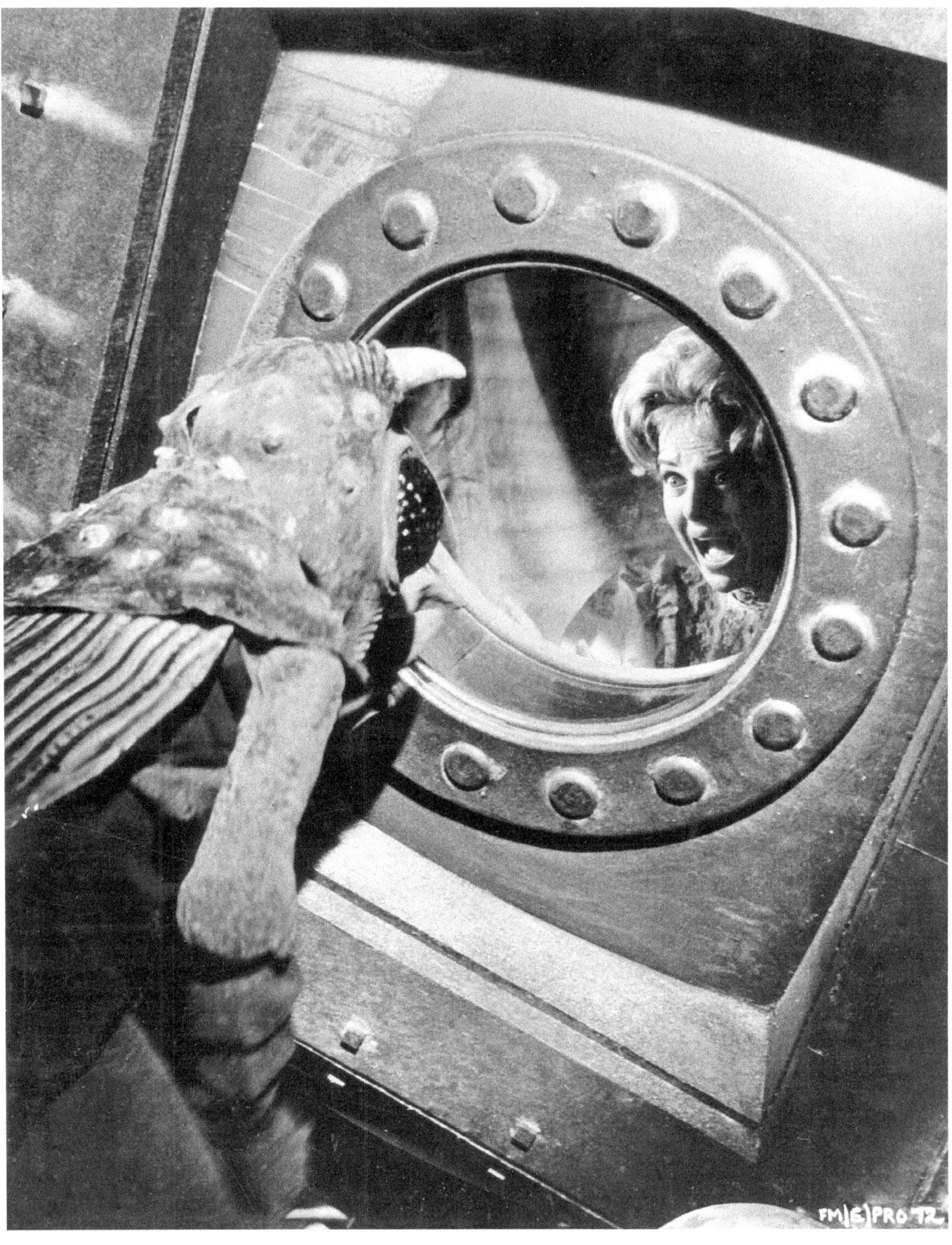

FIRST MEN IN THE MOON
Production: UK, 1964
Director: Nathan Juran
Category: Science Fiction

THE FORMS OF THINGS UNKNOWN
Production: USA, 1964
Director: Gerd Oswald
Category: Science Fiction/Horror

Originally filmed as a TV movie, but ultimately reconfigured as an episode of the classic SF TV show **The Outer Limits**, which ran from 1963 to 1965. David McCallum stars in a tale that combines elements of psycho-horror with meditations on time, death and resurrection. Director Gerd Oswald worked on some of the very best episodes of **The Outer Limits**, including **Demon With A Glass Hand** (also 1964), in which a man's artificial hand is a computer containing the data of every soul on Earth. Directed by Byron Haskin, written by Harlan Ellison and the recipient of a Hugo Award, **Demon With A Glass Hand** can be seen as an early glimmering of cyberpunk; it was filmed at the Bradbury Building in Los Angeles, where Ridley Scott would later shoot the climactic scenes of **Blade Runner**. Ellison also wrote the script and won a Hugo for the 1964 episode **Soldier** (again directed by Oswald), in which a fighter from the devastated earth of the future is sent back through time. Both episodes are believed to have heavily influenced James Cameron's **Terminator**, either directly or indirectly (through the 1966 production **Cyborg 2087**, which was most likely inspired by **The Outer Limits**.

LOVE GODDESSES OF BLOOD ISLAND
Production: USA, 1964
Director: Richard S. Flink
Alternative title: **Six Shes And A He**
Category: Science Fiction/Gore
One of the weirdest cult films of the early 1960s, a combination SF/sleaze/gore movie shot in Florida; the longest extant version runs at just under 50 minutes, during which we see an astronaut crash his ship on a desert island where he is assailed by six bikini-clad girls who apparently want him as a sex-toy. Since his predecessor ended up being bloodily decapitated and his head mounted on a stake (this is shown in a gruesome flashback), the stranded pilot has obviously got his work cut out. With its extreme gore effects mixed with elements of weird love, Flink's first and only film as director holds a unique position in the annals of trash.

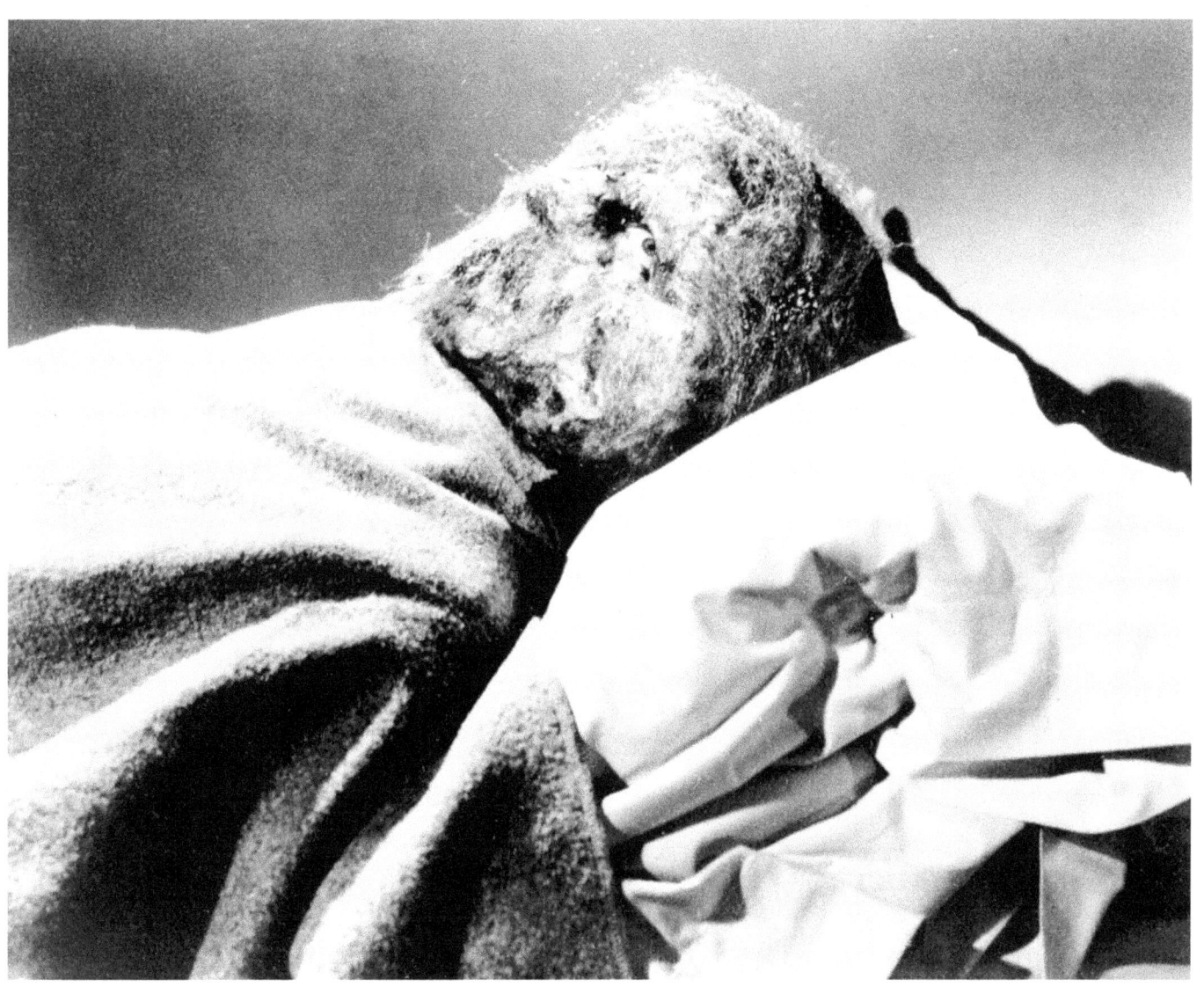

MUTINY IN OUTER SPACE
Production: USA, 1964
Director: Hugo Grimaldi
Category: Science Fiction

NAKED LUNCH
Production: UK, c.1964-72 (unfilmed)
Director: Antony Balch, Brion Gysin
Category: Science Fiction

Around 1964, Antony Balch and Brion Gysin made the first draft of a film script based on William S. Burroughs' novel *Naked Lunch*. Over subsequent years the script underwent several revisions, with text by Gysin and storyboards by Balch, until finally, in 1971, they – along with Burroughs – formed a production company specifically to film the project. In Gysin's story the action mostly takes place in Neverzone, where writer Bill Lee is hiding out after gunning down two narcotics cops, and also includes several routines by the famous Burroughs character Doctor Benway (supposedly to be played by Groucho Marx). Also involved are a pop act who incorporate live hangings in their show, as well as a murder-film which provokes autoerotic suicide in its audience. Despite interest from Mick Jagger, the film never got made, and it would be 20 years until David Cronenberg finally produced his own vision of the book.

SAN DAIKAIJU CHIKYU SAIDAI NO KESSEN
("Three Giant Monsters: Earth's Greatest Battle")
Production: Japan, 1964
Director: Ishiro Honda
English release title: **Ghidorah, The Three-Headed Monster**
Category: Science Fiction/Daikaiju

TIME TRAVELERS
Production: USA, 1964
Director: Ib Melchior
Category: Science Fiction

L'ULTIMO UOMO DELLA TERRA
("The Last Man Of Earth")
Production: Italy, 1964
Director: Ubaldo Ragona
Category: Science Fiction/Horror

Around 1961, Hammer Films had secured the film rights to Richard Matheson's classic novella *I Am Legend*, the story of the last man on earth persecuted by a nocturnal race of vampiric ghouls. Matheson himself prepared the script, but the project never came to fruition and one can only surmise that threatened censorship problems prevented the film – to be titled **Night Creatures** – being made. The book was subsequently filmed in Italy as **L'Ultimo Uomo Della Terra**, starring Vincent Price in the title role.

L'ÉTERNITÉ POUR NOUS
("Eternity For Us")
Production: France, 1963
Director: José Bénazéraf
Category: Sexploitation

SEX

AFRICA SEXY
Production: Italy, 1963
Director: Roberto Bianchi Montero
Category: Sexy Mondo

Montero's parade of ethnic, semi-nude dancers stands among the first in the "African" strain of Italian mondo movies that went on to encompass horrendous violence as well as sex. The director was churning out numerous voyeuristic documentaries in the early 60s, with the likes of **Universo Proibito, Sexy Nel Mondo, Sexy Nudo** and **Sexy Follie** all appearing in 1963 alone.

AMOK
Production: Greece, 1963
Director: Dinos Dimopoulos
Category: Sexploitation

A rare Greek sleaze item. Ten escaped female convicts are hiding out on a deserted island when seven men, led by a former Nazi, arrive looking for buried treasure. The women are forced to strip, are sexually assaulted, and then made to dig for the treasure, until they finally snap and bite back. Known as **The Rape** in the UK, and described by its distributors as "a hell of lust and violence".

BOIN-N-G
Production: USA, 1963
Director: Herchell Gordon Lewis
Category: Nudie-Cutie
"Undraped damsels by the dozens".

BUNNY YEAGER'S NUDE CAMERA
Production: USA, 1963
Director: Barry Mahon
Category: Nudie/Documentary
Nude model turned glamour photographer Yeager is filmed about her business, persuading buxotic young girls to strip and pose naked for the camera. Mahon and Yeager followed up with **Bunny Yeager's Nude Las Vegas** (1964); Yeager also appeared in Mahon's **Nudes On Tiger Reef** (1965).

THE CHRISTINE KEELER AFFAIR
Production: Denmark/UK, 1964
Director: Robert B. Spafford
Category: Sexploitation
Filmed to cash in on the notorious British political sex scandal known as the Profumo Affair,. It was banned from release by the UK censors and courts, and never commercially screened except in edited form overseas.

LE CITTÀ PROIBITE
("The Forbidden City")
Production: Italy, 1963
Director: Giuseppe Maria Scotese
Category: Mondo
Scotese's best contribution to the early 60s mondo explosion in Italy, with a focus on striptease and other glimpses of female nudity. The director had previously ventured into mondo territory with his documentaries **Questo Amore Ai Confini Del Mondo** (1960, with scenes of animal slaughter) and **America Di Notte** (1961, looking at striptease and other elements of "decadent" nightlife in the USA).

COCKS AND CUNTS
Production: USA, 1963
Director: Barbara Rubin
Alternative title: **Christmas On Earth**
Category: Sex/Underground
Not surprisingly, many of the most sexually explicit films produced during this period, apart from stag reels, emerged from the burgeoning underground art film scene. One of several underground films of the period to confront the viewer with exposed genitalia and explicit sex acts, Rubin's **Cocks And Cunts** presents a dual-projected polymorphous 29-minute orgy with masked, painted performers. Color filters and a random rock soundtrack made this a classic of transgressive expanded cinema. Some footage is said to have been shot in the apartment of future Velvet Underground catalyst John Cale, with whip-dancer Gerard Malanga among the participants.

FLAMING CREATURES
Production: USA, 1963
Director: Jack Smith
Category: Queer/Underground

"Is there a lipstick that doesn't come off when you suck cocks?" Thus asks director Jack Smith in the midst of his polymorphous perverse masterpiece, **Flaming Creatures**, the visual record of a transsexual orgy that culminates in cunnilingual rape. The creatures of the title, male, female, and in-between, and attired in garish exotic costumes, flash their genitals at certain points as they grope and cavort, glimpses which got the film banned and prosecuted in several cities. It all ends in a simulated earthquake. Smith never formally completed another film after **Flaming Creatures**, alhough he continued to shoot large amounts of footage; this would be constantly cut and recut in varying permutations and under different titles (such as **In The Grip Of The Lobster Claw** or **Zombie Of Uncle Pawnshop**), and used in expanded cinema events like Smith's 1965 cine-performance **Rehersal For The Destruction Of Atlantis**.

HOLLYWOOD'S WORLD OF FLESH
Production: USA, 1963
Director: Lee Frost
Category: Sexy Mondo

From Olymic International, this was Frost's first attempt at establishing a model for the American "mondo" movie, focusing on sex as much as possible. Highlights include the buxotic stripper Miss Baby Bubbles, who can also be seen in nudie-cuties **The Touchables** (1961) and Russ Meyer's **Exotica** (1961), as well as many burlesque loops of the period. Olympic International was a dstribution company started up around 1961 by Bob Cresse, handling domestic nudie-cutie films like **Babes In The Woods, House On Bare Mountain, It's Hot On Sin Island** and **Love Is A Four-Letter Word,** often with director Frost; the other films it released were a mixture of foreign imports, frequently cut with added sleaze scenes, and increasingly explicit home-grown exploitation items.

L'IMMORTELLE
("The Immortal Woman")
Production: France/Italy/Turkey, 1963
Director: Alain Robbe-Grillet
Category: Sexual Obsession

TA KOKKINA FANARIA
("The Red Lights")
Production: Greece, 1963
Director: Vasilis Georgiadis
English release title: **The Red Lanterns**
Category: Prostitution

MELLEM VENNER
("Between Friends")
Production: Denmark, 1963
Director: Poul Nyrup
Category: Sexploitation/Violence
Fast-moving and misogynistic, this tale of a young hoodlum/rapist named Kim and his wild drinking crew was purchased for distribution in the mid-60s by Radley Metzger's Audubon Films, who audaciously re-named it **Days Of Sin, Nights Of Nymphomania**, probably after splicing in additional scenes of female nudity. Importing racy foreign films, giving them even racier English titles, and re-editing them with additional shots of naked flesh was Audubon's main modus operandi.

NIHON NO YORU: ONNA ONNA ONNA MONOGATARI
("Night In Japan: Women Women Women Story")
Production: Japan, 1963
Director: Tetsuji Takechi
Category: Sexy Mondo
A "mondo"-style pseudo-documentary on Tokyo nightlife, predominantly focusing on striptease and naked female flesh. It was possibly inspired by Kelzo Ohno's nudie **Nihon No Yoru** (1962), and was in turn a direct inspiration for the unofficial sequel, **Shin Onna Onna Onna Monogatari** (Taijiro Tamura, 1964). The history of Japanese "sex mondo" movies can be traced back to clandestine 50s films such as **Sutorippu Tokyo** and **Sekai Kakkoku No Seihokoku**.

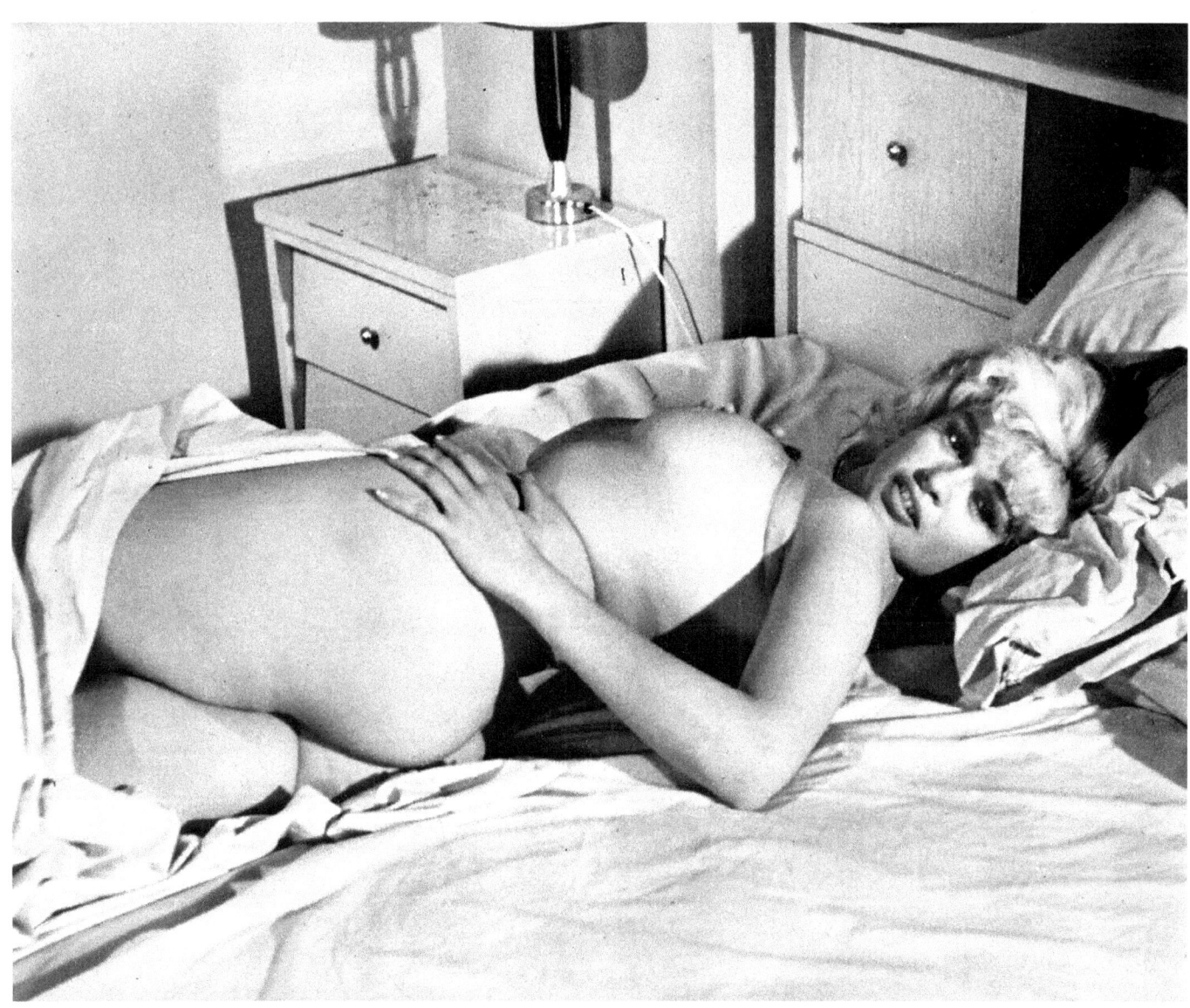

PROMISES! PROMISES!
Production: USA, 1963
Director: King Donovan
Category: Sexploitation
The film in which Jayne Mansfield finally strips nude for the movie camera, revealing her amazing body to all the world – the first time a leading Hollywood

star had done so; this happens early in the film, and the rest is just a forgettable comedy. Although the nudity is confined to a few brief bathroom scenes, a revealing promotional spread in *Playboy* ensured the film was a huge novelty hit. Mansfield's nude scenes were also released on an 8mm glamour reel for home viewing, and touted as "The most BANNED! BARED! and BARRED film ever!" Co-star Tommy Noonan later worked with another blonde sex-bomb, directing Mamie Van Doren in the screwy comedy **3 Nuts In Search Of A Bolt** (1964).

PSYCHOMONTAGE
Production: USA, 1963
Director: Eberhard & Phyllis Kronhausen
Category: Sexology
Pioneering sexologists the Kronhausens present a film comprised of stock footage designed to show how any visual stimulus can arouse the viewer and appear erotic. the couples' later films included the permissive sex drama **Freedom To Love** (1969), and **Sex Circus** (1973), in which a circus seeks to boost its revenue by including live shows of dwarfs and animals copulating (though not each other).

SCUM OF THE EARTH
Production: USA, 1963
Director: Hercshell Gordon Lewis
Category: Sex Roughie

Often cited as the prototype for the "roughie", a 60s movie sub-genre predominantly featuring violence against women, with as much nudity as the film-makers could get away with. Deliberately shot crudely on 16mm black-and-white stock to recreate the feel of a stag movie, **Scum Of The Earth** concerns a pornography ring involved in the blackmail, beating and rape of young female victims. It was released in nude and non-nude versions, and also known as **Devil's Camera**.

SHOTGUN WEDDING
Production: USA, 1963
Director: Boris Petroff
Category: Sexploitation

SITTLICHKEITSVERBRECHER
("Sex Offender")
Production: Germany, 1963
Director: Franz Schnyder
English release title: **The Molesters**
Category: Sex Roughie

SPREE

Production: USA, 1963/67
Director: Mitchell Leisen, Walon Green
Category: Documentary

A mondo-style documentary on the "sexy' nightlife of Las Vegas, filmed primarily at the Tropicana Hotel and Dunes Hotel in 1962-63. Various stars are shown performing musical numbers, and Jayne Mansfield features in her famous quasi-striptease routine. **Spree** also includes scenes of gambling casinos, cock fights and boxing; the film's lurid publicity hinted at demonic possession, strange fetishes, feral women, and "uninhibited" behaviour. Mansfield also appeared in Luigi Scattini's **Amore Primitivo** (Italy, 1964), an odd combination of sex farce and sex mondo movie, in which she plays an anthropologist who shows footage of primitive culture and mating rituals – including nudity and the killing of live animals – to a guest. An odd Italian comedy duo also appear, and Jayne herself does a couple of music/striptease routines.

STRIP-TEASE
Production: France, 1963
Director: Jacques Poitrenaud
Category: Striptease Culture

Velvet Underground vocalist Nico (credited as Krista Nico) made an early film appearance in this rare, raunchy but serious-minded French film about a career dancer who turns to stripping to make money. She also recorded a version of the film's title song, written by Serge Gainsbourg, but it was re-recorded for release by Juliette Greco. A year later she met Brian Jones and made her first single for Andrew Loog Oldham's Immediate label, produced by Jimmy Page. Nico's next significant film appearances would be in movies by Andy Warhol.

TAKE OFF YOUR CLOTHES AND LIVE!
Production: UK, 1963
Director: Arthur Lewis Miller
Category: Nudism

VIOLATED PARADISE
Production: Japan/Italy/USA, 1963
Director: Marion Gering
Alternative title: **Diving Girls Of Japan**
Category: Sexy Mondo
Cultural documentary presenting a mondo-style look at a modern "*geisha*" girl travelling through Japan in search of employment. Various Tokyo entertainment establishments are featured, all with topless girls. Our *geisha* finally finds work as a pearl diver (another topless line of work). Although intended as a more serious-minded report, Gering's film was marketed as sexploitation and released on a double bill with the Barry Mahon nudie-cutie **1,000 Shapes Of A Female** (also 1963).

WILD IS MY LOVE
Production: USA, 1963
Director: Richard Hilliard
Category: Sexploitation
Sleazy drama involving a youth-corrupting stripper, distributed by William Mishkin.

A WOLF'S STORY
Production: USA, c.1963-66
Director: Anonymous
Category: Pornography
An unusual horror-themed adults-only stag movie, showing an array of sex acts and perversions and bizarrely featuring a male and female werewolf.

THE YELLOW TEDDY BEARS
Production: UK, 1963
Director: Robert Hartford-Davis
US release title: **Gutter Girls**
Category: Sexploitation
Sleazy British "message" movie dealing with aspects of underage sex, specifically a clique of schoolgirls who wear teddy bear badges to signify the loss of their virginity. It focuses on one girl, Linda, who has to deal with an unwanted pregnancy and back-street abortionists in a rather grim reminder of repressive England before the 60s started to swing.

ACOSADA

Production: Argentina/Venezuela, 1964
Director: Alberto Dubois
US release title: **The Pink Pussy: Where Sin Lives**
Category: White Slavery

Rare exploitation movie from South America, about a girl in New York who signs a contract to work in Caracas, but ends up being beaten, raped, and thrust into white slavery. Dubois' previous film **La Flor de Irupé** (1962), a lurid swamp movie, was also picked up for US distribution, and retitled **Love Hunger** after the insertion of a 12-minute colour sequence of nude girls. Another white slavery film was Georges Combret's **La Traite Des Blanches** ("The White Woman Trade"), which was imported to the US by Audubon and released under the title **Hot Frustrations** in 1965, most likely with new erotic inserts.

ÄLSKANDE PAR
("Loving Couples")
Production: Sweden, 1964
Director: Mai Zetterling
Category: Sexology
Three pregnant women reflect on how they came to be in their present position, their discussion centring around sexual matters. Pregnancy, sexual fulfillment, sexual repression, adultery, premarital sex, lesbianism, male homosexuality, bisexuality and paedophilia are all featured, boosting director Zetterling's reputation as a taboo-breaker, a sexually-explicit female Ingmar Bergman. This notoriety would peak with her next film, the depraved Freudian inferno **Nattlek**.

ANGELIC FRANKENSTEIN
Production: USA, 1964
Director: Bob Mizer
Category: Homoerotic
Short queer movie in which Frankenstein creates a perfect male lover from a doll. But when he tries to teach him to shoot guns, the creatures attacks him and runs away. Another queer short "inspired by" the same horror classic was **Hollow-My-Weenie, Dr. Frankenstein** (1969), a sex film involving the doctor, his hunch-backed assistant, and the well-endowed monster they create in the laboratory. Bob Mizer was the founder, in 1945, of the Athletic Model Guild (AMG) and its magazine *Physique Pictorial*, which published gay photography thinly disguised as "physical culture". AMG first went into commercial film in the 1950s, producing camp homoerotic dramas with titles like **Aztec Sacrifice** or **Boy Slaves For Sale**, and duly moved into hardcore in the 1970s, with such entries as **Cowboy Virgin** and the SM orgy **Night In A Dungeon** (although AMG-produced hardcore stag reels for private consumption, such as **Shore Leave**, date back as far as 1945). Joe Dallesandro and Arnold Schwarzenegger were among the many aspiring actors who posed for AMG photograph sessions. Homosexuality was rarely addressed in standard sexploitation films of the early 60s, although it is a factor in one part of Robert Stambler's **Strange Lovers**, released in 1963.

LA BAIE DU DÉSIR
("Bay Of Desire")
Production: France, 1964
Director: Max Pécas
Category: Sexploitation
A sexy thriller imported for US distribution by Audubon Films, boosted by inserts of nude woman filmed by Radley Metzger, and released as **The Erotic Touch Of Hot Skin** in 1966. Audubon released another film by Max Pécas, **Douce Violence** (1962), under the US title **Sweet Ecstasy**. They also distributed domestic productions in the sexploitation genre, such as Joe Sarno's **Warm Nights And Hot Pleasures** (1964).

BODY OF A FEMALE
Production: USA, 1964
Director: John Amero, Michael Findlay
Category: Sex Roughie
A stripper is kidnapped and whipped by a jaded libertine. This film is noteworthy as being the first to give directorial credit to Michael Findlay (as Julian Marsh), who went on to be a key director in adult films. His wife Roberta (as Anna Riva) plays the stripper.

BUNNY YEAGER'S NUDE LAS VEGAS
Production: USA, 1964
Director: Barry Mahon
Category: Nudie

CARESSED
Production: Canada, 1964
Director: Larry Kent
Original title: **Sweet Substitute**
Category: Sexploitation
Picked up and retitled for US distribution by Joseph Brenner, this tale of teenage lust involves free love, lesbianism and unwanted pregnancy.

CINQ FILLES EN FURIE
("Five Enraged Girls")
Production: France, 1964
Director: Max Pécas
Category: Sexploitation

Five young women, on vacation in southern France and staying at an old mansion, are led to believe that Nazi treasure is buried nearby, and try to cajole its location from Martha, a local drunk. They also enlist the help of two men, giving plenty of opportunity for scenes of seduction and nudity. At the film's brutal climax, a confrontation with Martha reveals that she accidentally dropped and thereby killed a child belonging to one of the girls; after this revelation, she kills herself by leaping from a balcony. This sleazy mixture of crime, sex, avarice and death was just one of many exploitational films directed in the 60s by Pécas, the doyen of French "Z" movies, or *cinéma nanard*; most Pécas movies were produced by his own company, Les Films du Griffon. Pécas later moved into straight erotica, with entries like **Je Suis Une Nymphomane** (1970), and graduated to hardcore as soon as it was legalized in France.

COVER GIRLS
Production: Italy/France, 1964
Director: José Bénazéraf
Category: Sexploitation

DIRTY GIRLS
Production: USA, 1964
Director: Radley Metzger
Category: Sexploitation
Released in early 1965, Metzger's second film is a study of European prostitutes, shot in Paris and Munich. (His first film, **Dictionary Of Sex,** appears to be more of a compilation of erotic scenes from other sources, mainly foreign imports).

FANNY HILL: MEMORIES OF A WOMAN OF PLEASURE
Production: USA/Germany, 1964
Director: Russ Meyer, Albert Zugsmith
Category: Sexploitation

It was during his classic early "roughie" period that Russ Meyer became involved, incongruously, with Albert Zugsmith's production of the erotic novel *Fanny Hill*, filmed in Germany. As if to confirm his own mistake in becoming involved, Meyer abandoned this project before completion, leaving Zugsmith to finish directorial duties himself. Meyer ultimately disowned the film, which ended up as an inane, sexless romp, but the mantle was soon taken up by fellow nudie-doyen Barry Mahon, who produced the demented softcore trilogy **Fanny Hill Meets Dr. Erotico**, **Fanny Hill Meets The Red Baron**, and **Fanny Hill Meets Lady Chatterley's Lover**, while Peter Perry contributed **The Notorious Daughter Of Fanny Hill** (1966) to this shadowy list. Perry's film, produced by David Friedman, featured a blonde hooker named Kissy Hill whose clients include the masochistic Count de Sade. Swedish director Mac Ahlberg brought out his own **Fanny Hill** in 1968, and back in the USA in 1971, Joe Sarno created a sleazy, lesbian-oriented modern update set in Manhattan, **The Young And Erotic Fanny Hill**.

LA FEMME SPECTACLE
("The Woman Show")
Production: France, 1964
Director: Claude Lelouch
US release title: Paris In the Raw
Category: Documentary
A mondo-style compendium of footage concerning women, including childbirth and suicide.

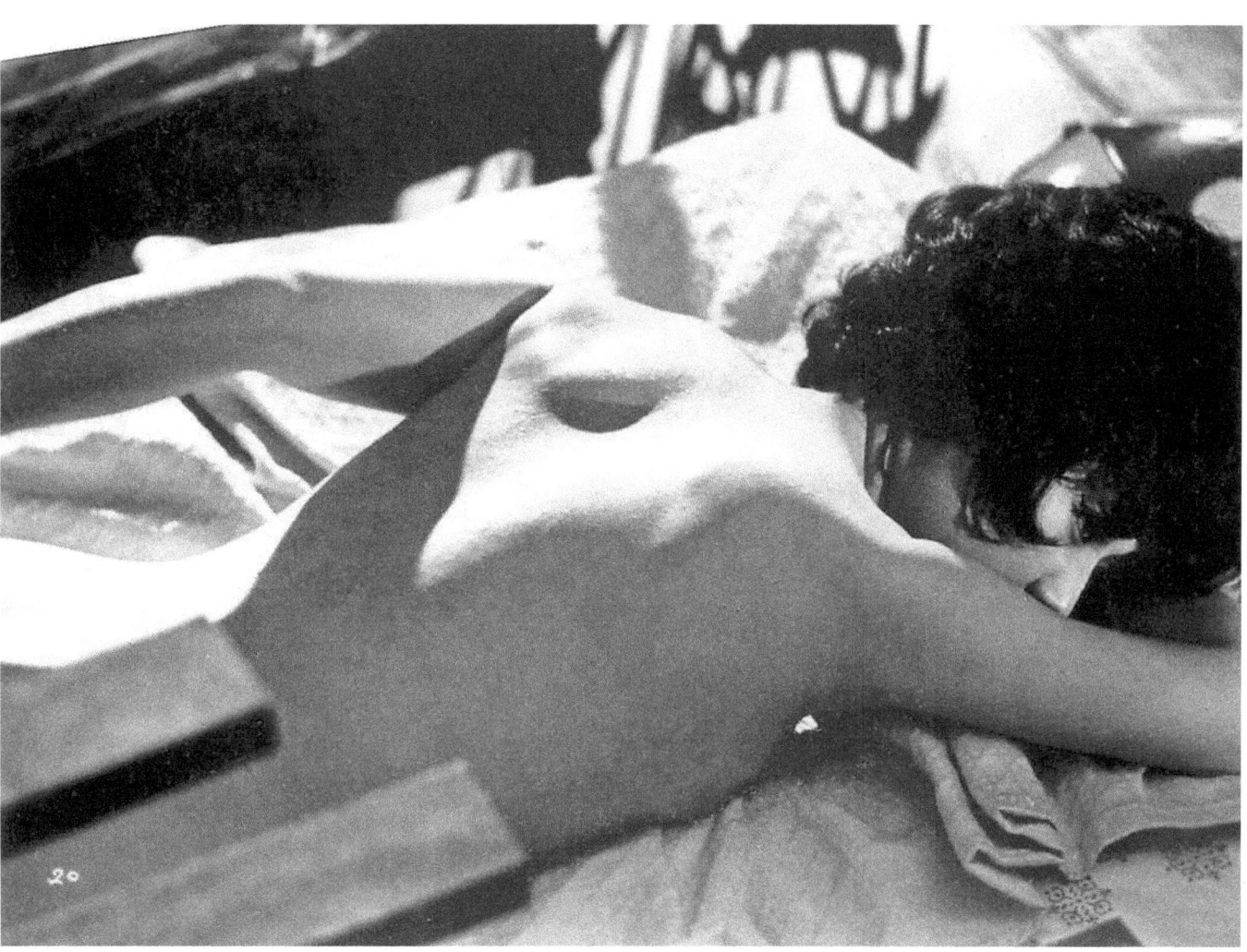

HAKUJITSUMU
("Daydream")
Production: Japan, 1964
Director: Tetsuji Takechi
Category: Erotic
A landmark in the development of *pinku eiga* ("pink film"), a term popularized by Japanese production companies to promote the line of sexploitation movies they developed in the 1960s to the early 1970s. **Hakujitsumu** is generally considered to be the first historically significant movie in the genre, with director Takechi regarded as the "Godfather of Japanese porno cinema". Produced by Shochiku Studios, this was the first of the so-called "Japanese New Wave" films to present a blatantly erotic storyline, featuring female nudity and even a brief glimpse of armpit and

pubic hair, very much taboo in Japanese society. The "daydream" of the film's title is experienced by a young artist whilst under anaesthesia at his dentist's. He hallucinates about a pretty young girl whom he met in the waiting-room, seeing her subjected to all kinds of sexual molestation, rape and torture by the sadistic dentist. This includes hanging her from the ceiling and electric shock treatment. When he wakes up, the reality – or otherwise – of his voyeuristic experience becomes ambiguous. Guaranteed wide distribution by dint of deriving from a work by popular, respected novelist Junichiro Tanizaki, **Hakujitsumu** opened at the same time as the Tokyo Olympics, causing much embarassment to the Japanese government, who strongly objected to the "amoral" image of their nation the film might give to the rest of the world. **Hakujitsumu** was eventually distributed in America by exploitation filmmaker Joseph Green (director of **The Brain That Wouldn't Die**, 1959), who shot and spliced in additional psychedelic dream sequences for a 1966 release. **Chunmong** was a 1965 Koerean remake by director Yu Hyun-mok, who was arrested for indecency. Takechi's next erotic film, **Kokeimu**, was also released in 1964, but only after some 20% of its content was cut and destroyed by the Japanese censor.

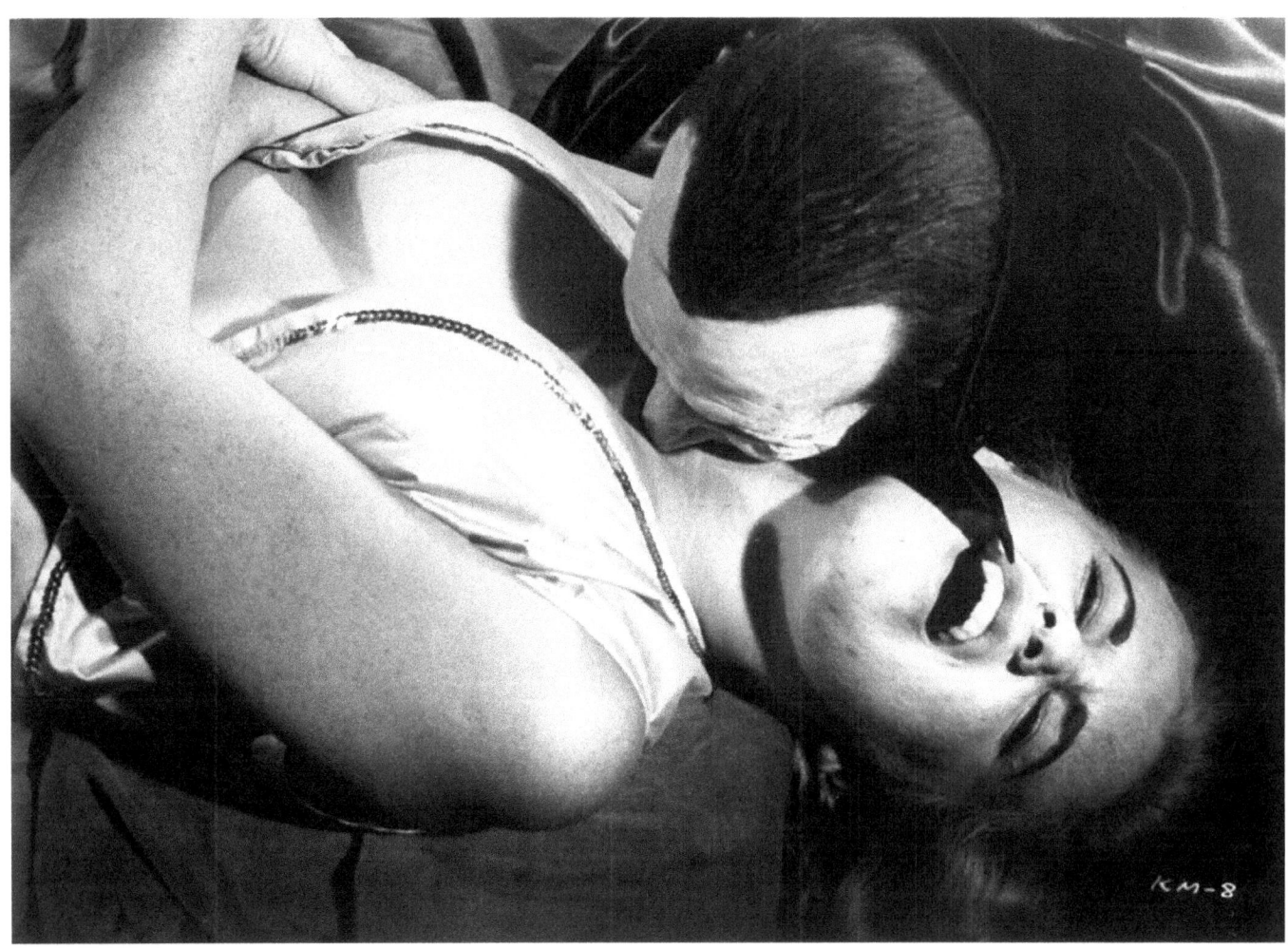

KISS ME QUICK
Production: USA, 1964
Director: Peter Perry
Category: Nudie/Science Fiction

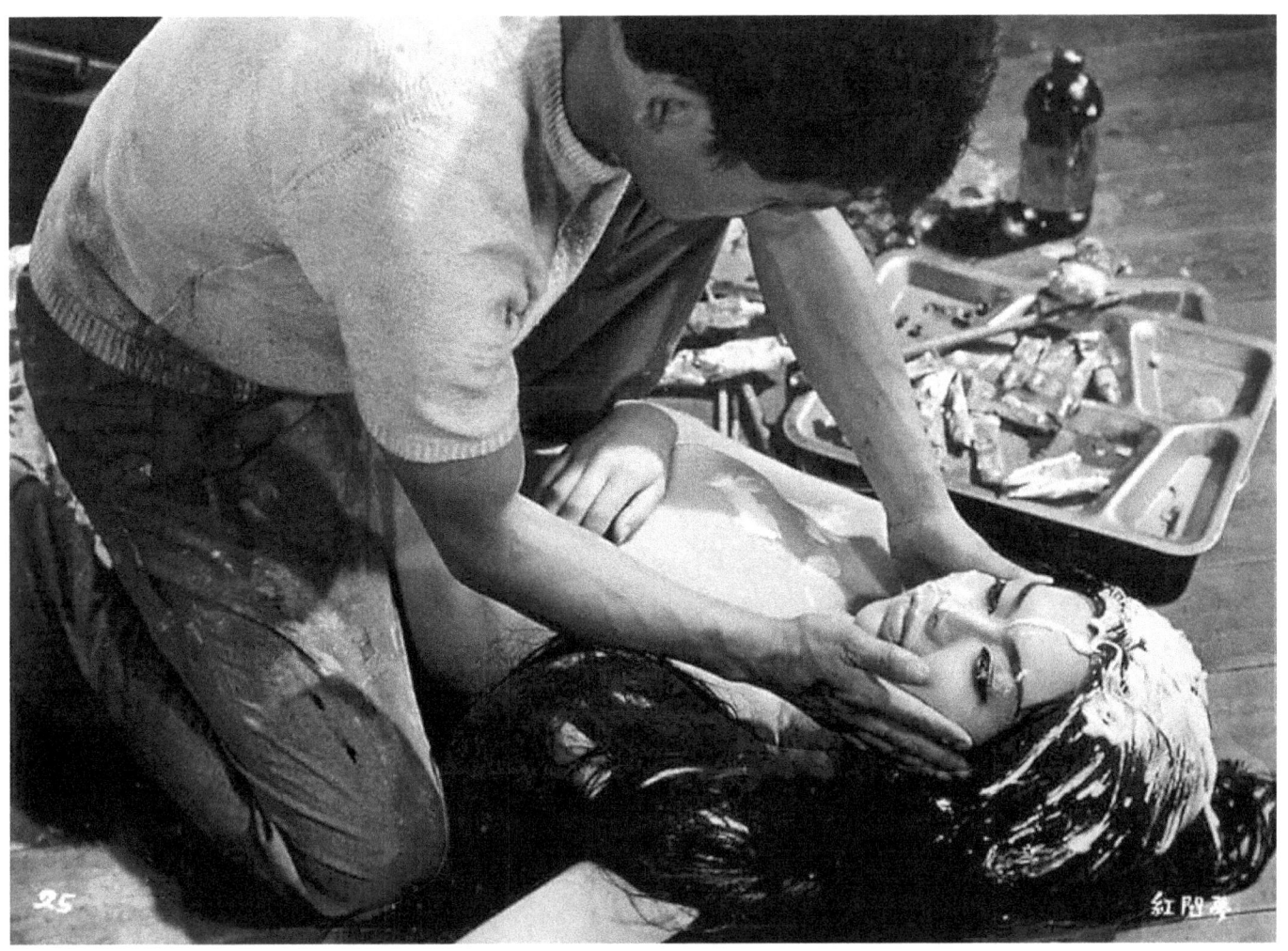

KOKEIMU
("Crimson Dream")
Production: Japan, 1964
Director: Tetsuji Takechi
Category: Erotic

LONDON IN THE RAW
Production: UK, 1964
Director: Arnold Louis Miller
Category: Documentary

British exploitation mogul Miller – known for nudist films such as **Nudes Of The World** and **Nudist Memories** – brought out **West End Jungle**, a sensationalistic glimpse into the underbelly of London's Soho, in 1961. **London In The Raw** is a sequel, with more footage shot in seedy bars, casinos, strip clubs and lounges. Miller followed up with a third in this "mondo"-type series, **Primitive London**, in 1965, featuring youth fashions and other diversions. The first feature-length film to show nude scenes from Soho's demi-monde was probably Roger Proudlock's **Soho Striptease** (1960), filmed at the legendary Gargoyle Club. Also of interest are the short documentaries **Carousella** (John Irvin, 1965) and **Strip** (Peter Davis, Staffan Lamm, and Don DeFina, 1965).

LORNA

Production: USA, 1964
Director: Russ Meyer
Category: Sex Roughie

The advent of the "roughie" marks a progression in sex cinema from the relatively harmless nudie-cutie format to something more pernicious. This new genre of sexploitation offered the audience kicks derived from the sight of women being slapped around, beaten, raped, and even tortured. **Lorna**, a rural roughie, was Meyer's first foray into this arena.

MY TALE IS HOT

Production: USA, 1964
Director: Peter Perry
Category: Nudie

Probably the first Satanic nudie film, starring legendary stripper Candy Barr in a romp with the Devil, who tries his best to tempt a pious husband into adultery. Perry had previously directed what was probably the first nudie Western, **Revenge Of The Virgins** (1959, scripted by Ed Wood, Jr.), possibly the first nudie horror film, **Honeymoon Of Terror** (1961), and definitely not the first nudie SF film, **Knockers Up** (1963).

NIKUTAI NO MON
("Gate Of Flesh")
Production: Japan, 1964
Director: Seijun Suzuki
Category: Sexploitation
Suzuki's drama deals with a band of Tokyo prostitutes in the aftermath of WW2, with some scenes of bondage and nudity. The following year he directed **Shunpuden** ("Prostitute Story"), this time set during the war itself and dealing with the plight of "comfort women" on the Manchurian front, and completed this loose trilogy with **Kawachi Karumen** ("Kawachi Carmen", 1966).

OLGA

Production: USA, 1964-66
Director: Joseph Mawra
Category: Sexploitation

Produced by George Weiss, the **Olga** movies are notorious landmarks in the development of 60s sexploitation cinema, infamous for their then-unprecedented depictions of the torture and abuse of women. The original trilogy commenced in 1964 with **White Slaves Of Chinatown**, and continued with **Olga's Girls** and **Olga's House Of Shame**. **Madame Olga's Massage Parlor** was an unoffical sequel from 1965. Mawra also used clips from most of the films in the "fake" documentary **Mondo Oscenita** (1966), a film ostensibly detailing the rise in sexual violence in exploitation films, but actually acting as a free advert for the **Olga** series. **Olga's Dance Hall Girls** (1969) was a late and final entry.

ORGY OF THE GOLDEN NUDES

Production: USA, 1964
Director: Irwin Meyer
Category: Sexploitation

A prime example of sexploitative cinema, **Orgy Of The Golden Nudes** was a version of the psycho-horror movie **Honeymoon Of Horror** with new footage of female nudity cut in. The main atttraction of these additional sequences was Gigi Darlene, an early sex star who performed as a stripper, nude model, and nude actress. Her earlier credits included sleazy nude model inserts in **The Unsatisfied** – the US release of Spanish JD film **Juventud A La Intemperie** ("Youth Exposed", 1961).

PARIS SECRET
("Secret Paris")
Production: France, 1964
Director: Edouard Logereau
Category: Mondo
Maybe the first French mondo movie, this clandestine glimpse at the dark side of the French capital includes scenes of circus freaks, corpses illegally imported for medical experimentation, animal slaughter, a Satanic black mass and, of course, naked women being tattooed.

PASSION IN THE SUN
Production: USA, 1964
Director: Dale Berry
Category: Nudie/Horror
A denizen of ultra-low-budget sexploitation cinema of the mid-60s, Dale Berry is known to have directed at least four features, of which **Passion In The Sun** – sometimes referred to as **The Girl And The Geek** – is the first. It features as many topless nude scenes as possible, achieved by crafting a story in which a busty stripper is abducted by gangsters, escapes and goes swimming in the woods, but is then stalked by an escaped sub-normal carnival freak, who at one point rips off her blouse. The film climaxes in an amusement park, with the geek finally killed when he's struck by the stripper's ride car (the ride featured in the film, a "Wild Mouse" rollercoaster as designed by Franz Mack of Germany in 1957, is also of considerable interest to vintage arcade enthusiasts). A primitive amalgam of nudie-cutie and freak film, a formula not to be lightly dismissed despite the first-time director's ineptitude. Berry's next film, **Hot-Blooded Woman** (1965), concerned a stripper committed to a lunatic asylum for attempted murder and wanton nudity. He also directed **Hot Thrills And Warm Chills** and **Hip Hot And 21** (both 1967), and scripted in starred in **The Hot Bed** (1965), amongst other bargain buys of the cheap sleaze sinema.

SINDERELLA AND THE GOLDEN BRA
Production: USA, 1964
Director: Loel Minardi
Category: Nudie Fantasy
Nudie feature based on the classic fairy tale "Cinderella" but swapping the slipper for a bra, with much baring of ample female breasts as all the girls try on the golden garment to see which tits it fits.

SUNA NO ONNA
("Woman Of The Sands")
Production: Japan, 1964
Director: Hiroshi Teshigahara
Category: Arthouse
This serious film presents an exercise in claustrophobic eroticism in which an entomologist finds himself stranded in the sand-swamped house of a sexually voracious widow. Initially held against his will by other village-folk, he eventually accepts this new life, as meaningless as any other. The copulation scenes use extreme close-ups, making the woman's skin resemble the lunar surface and rendering the sex act in monstrous abstract.

3 NUTS IN SEARCH OF A BOLT
Production: USA, 1964
Director: Tommy Noonan
Category: Sex Comedy
Pseudo-nudie screwball farce, notable only for its publicity shots showing a rear shot of the sensational Mamie Van Doren nude on screen for the first time, albeit in an extremely brief bubble-bath scene. However, her naked buttocks are not fully exposed in the final version. Noonan doubtless got the idea after acting in **Promises Promises** (1963), in which Jayne Mansfield also made her naked debut on film.

INDEX OF MAIN TITLES

MEIA-NOITE LEVAREI SUA ALMA (1963-64)	8-9, 8
A PATY JEZDEC JE STRACH (1964)	79
ACOSADA (1964)	157
THE ADDAMS FAMILY (1964-66)	32, 33
AFRICA SEXY (1963)	142
AIMEZ-VOUS DES FEMMES? (1964)	80
ÄLSKANDE PAR (1964)	158
AMOK (1963)	142, 142-143
ANGELIC FRANKENSTEIN (1964)	158
LA BAIE DU DÉSIR (1964)	158, 159
BAKUMATSU ZANKOKU MONOGATARI (1964)	105
THE BEAUTIFUL, THE BLOODY, AND THE BARE (1964)	80
THE BIRDS (1963)	9
THE BLACK TORMENT (1964)	33
BLACK ZOO (1963)	10
BLOOD FEAST (1963)	11
BODY OF A FEMALE (1964)	160
BOIN-N-G (1963)	143
BUNNY YEAGER'S NUDE CAMERA (1963)	144
BUNNY YEAGER'S NUDE LAS VEGAS (1964)	161
BYLEM KAPO (1964)	81
CARESSED (1964)	162
IL CASTELLO DEI MORTI VIVENTI (1964)	34
THE CHAIR (1963)	60
THE CHILD MOLESTER (1964)	81
CHILDREN OF THE DAMNED (1964)	128
THE CHRISTINE KEELER AFFAIR (1963)	144
CINQ FILLES EN FURIE (1964)	163
LE CITTÀ PROIBITE (1963)	144
COCKS AND CUNTS (1963)	144
THE COOL WORLD (1963)	60, 60-61
COVER GIRLS (1964)	164
CURSE OF SIMBA (1964)	35
CURSE OF THE LIVING CORPSE (1964)	36
CURSE OF THE MUMMY'S TOMB (1964)	36, 37
DANZA MACABRA (1964)	38
THE DAY OF THE TRIFFIDS (1963)	118, 119
DEMENTIA 13 (1963)	12
IL DEMONIO (1963)	13
DEUS E O DIABO NA TERRA DO SOL (1964)	106, 106-107
THE DEVIL DOLL (1964)	39
DEVIL WOLF OF SHADOW MOUNTAIN (1964)	39
I DIECI GLADIATORI (1963)	100
DIRTY GIRLS (1964)	165
DOCTOR TERROR'S HOUSE OF HORRORS (1964)	40
DOCTOR WHO (1963)	120
LA DONNA SCIMMIA (1963)	61
DUNGEONS OF HORROR (1963)	14
THE EARTH DIES SCREAMING (1964)	128, 129
ECCO (1963)	62

EINER FRISST DEN ANDEREN (1963-64)	62-63, 63
L'ÉTERNITÉ POUR NOUS (1963)	140, 141
EVIL OF FRANKENSTEIN (1964)	41
FACE OF THE SCREAMING WEREWOLF (1964)	42
FANNY HILL: MEMORIES OF A WOMAN OF PLEASURE (1964)	166
LA FEMME SPECTACLE (1964)	167
A FINNISH FABLE (1963)	100-101
FIRST MEN IN THE MOON (1964)	130, 131
FLAMING CREATURES (1963)	145
DER FLUCH DER GRÜNEN AUGEN (1964)	43
THE FORMS OF THINGS UNKNOWN (1964)	133, 134
LA FRUSTA E IL CORPO (1963)	14-15, 14
FUEGO (1964)	44
GESTAPOMAN SCHMIDT (1964)	81
GOLDFINGER (1964)	107, 107-108
THE GORGON (1964)	3, 44-45, 45
LA GRANDE FROUSSE (1964)	81-82
HAKUJITSUMU (1960)	167, 167-168
THE HAUNTED PALACE (1963)	15
THE HAUNTING (1963)	16, 17
DER HENKER VON LONDON (1963)	64
HOLLYWOOD'S WORLD OF FLESH (1963)	146
HORROR (1963)	17
HORROR AT PARTY BEACH (1964)	46
HOUSE OF THE DAMNED (1963)	18
HYSTERIA (1964)	82
IKARIE XB1 (1963)	121
THE INCREDIBLY STRANGE CREATURES WHO STOPPED LIVING AND BECAME CRAZY MIXED-UP ZOMBIES (1963-64)	19
LA INVASIÓN DE LOS VAMPIROS (1963)	20
GLI INVINCIBILI DIECI GLADIATORI (1964)	108
JASON AND THE ARGONAUTS (1963)	101
L'IMMORTELLE (1963)	146
JUDEX (1963)	65
KAIDAN (1964)	47
KAIDAN ONI-BI NO NUMA (1963)	6, 7
KAITEI GUNKAN (1963)	122
KALEIDOSCOPE (1964-67)	83
KATARSIS (1963)	20
KAWAITA HANA (1964)	83, 83-84
THE KILLERS (1964)	84
KISS ME QUICK (1964)	168
KISS OF THE VAMPIRE (1963)	21
KITTEN WITH A WHIP (1964)	85
KOKEIMU (1964)	169
TA KOKKINA FANARIA (1963)	147
KULAY DUGO ANG GABI (1964)	48
KUNOICHI NINPO (1964)	109
KWAHERI: VANISHING AFRICA (1964)	85
LABIRYNT (1963)	102
LONDON IN THE RAW (1964)	169
LORD OF THE FLIES (1963)	66
LORNA (1964)	3, 170
LOVE GODDESSES OF BLOOD ISLAND (1964)	134
LAS LUCHADORAS CONTRA EL MÉDICO ASESINO (1963)	22
I LUNGHI CAPELLI DELLA MORTE (1964)	49
MACISTE CONTRO I MONGOLI 1963)	98, 99
MACISTE E LA REGINA DI SAMAR (1964)	110
MACISTE L'EROE PIÙ GRANDE DEL MONDO (1963)	102
THE MADMEN OF MANDORAS (1963)	123
LA MALDICIÓN DE LA LLORONA (1963)	23
MANIAC (1963)	67
THE MASQUE OF THE RED DEATH (1964)	2, 50
MATANGO (1963)	124
MELLEM VENNER (1963)	147
METEMPSYCHO (1963)	24

MOB AND RIOT CONTROL (1964)	85-86
MONDO BALORDO (1964)	86
MONSTROSITY (1963)	25
IL MOSTRO DELL'OPERA (1964)	51
MUTINY IN OUTER SPACE (1964)	135
MY TALE IS HOT (1964)	170
THE NAKED KISS (1964)	86
NAKED LUNCH (c.1964-1972)	135-136
THE NAKED WITCH (1964)	51
NEMURI KYOSHIRO SAPPOCHO (1963)	103
THE NIGHT WALKER (1964)	52
NIGHTMARE (1964)	87
NIHON NO YORU: ONNA ONNA ONNA MONOGATARI (1963)	148
NIHON ZANKOKU MONOGATARI (1963)	67-68
NIKUTAI NO MON (1964)	171
DIE NYLONSCHLINGE (1963)	68
OLGA (1964-66)	172, 173
ONIBABA (1964)	53, 53-54
ORGY OF THE GOLDEN NUDES (1964)	173, 173-174
OTOKO NO MONSHO (1963)	58, **59**
PARANOIAC (1963)	69
PARIS SECRET (1964)	174
PARQUE DE JUEGOS (1963)	26
PASSION IN THE SUN (1964)	174
PER UN PUGNO DI DOLLARI (1964)	111
DAS PHANTOM VON SOHO (1964)	88
PROMISES! PROMISES! (1963)	148, 148-149
PSYCHOMONTAGE (1963)	149
QUESTO MONDO PROIBITO (1963)	70
LA RAGAZZA CHE SAPEVA TROPPO (1963)	71
LA RIVOLTA DEI SETTE (1964)	112, **113**
ROMA CONTRO ROMA (1964)	113
ROSTRO INFERNAL (1963)	27
THE SADIST (1963)	72, 72-73
SAN DAIKAIJU CHIKYU SAIDAI NO KESSEN (1964)	136
DER SCHWARZE ABT (1963)	73
GLI SCHIAVI PIÙ FORTI DEL MONDO (1964)	114
SCUM OF THE EARTH (1963)	149, 149-150
SEI DONNE PER L'ASSASSINO (1964)	1, 89
7 FACES OF DR. LAO (1964)	115
SHADES AND DRUMBEATS (1964)	89
SHOCK CORRIDOR (1963)	74
SHOCK TREATMENT (1964)	90
SHOTGUN WEDDING (1963)	150
SINDERELLA AND THE GOLDEN BRA (1964)	175
SITTLICHKEITSVERBRECHER (1963)	151
THE SLIME PEOPLE (1963)	125
LO SPETTRO (1963)	27
SPREE (1963/67)	152
SPIDER BABY (1964)	54, 54-55
STRAITJACKET (1964)	91
THE STRANGLER (1964)	92
STRIP-TEASE (1963)	153
SUNA NO ONNA (1964)	176
TABETA HITO (1963)	75
I TABÙ (1963)	75
TAKE OFF YOUR CLOTHES AND LIVE! (1963)	154
THE TERROR (1963)	28
3 NUTS IN SEARCH OF A BOLT (1964)	176, 177
THE THRILL KILLERS (1964)	93
LE TIGRE AIME LA CHAIR FRAÎCHE (1964)	116
TIME TRAVELERS (1964)	137
THE TOMB OF LIGEIA (1964)	55
TOWERS OPEN FIRE (1963)	125
I TRE VOLTI DELLA PAURA (1963)	29
THE TRIAL OF LEE HARVEY OSWALD (1964)	93

TWICE-TOLD TALES (1963)	30
TWO ON A GUILLOTINE (1964)	94
TWO THOUSAND MANIACS (1964)	95
L'ULTIMO UOMO DELLA TERRA (1964)	**138, 139**
UNEARTHLY STRANGER (1963)	**126**
DAS UNGEHEUER VON LONDON CITY (1964)	**96**, 97
UNTITLED [THE HANGING FILMS OF ANATOLY SLIVKO] (1964-85)	97
LA VERGINE DI NORIMBERGA (1963)	**31**
VIOLATED PARADISE (1963)	155
DIE WEISSE SPINNE (1963)	**76**
WHEELS OF TRAGEDY (1963)	77
WILD IS MY LOVE (1963)	**155**
WITCHCRAFT (1964)	**56**
A WOLF'S STORY (c.1963-66)	156
DER WÜRGER VON SCHLOSS BLACKMOOR (1963)	77
X (1963)	**127**
YAJU NO SEISHUN (1963)	**78**
THE YELLOW TEDDY BEARS (1963)	**156**
YUKINOJO HENGE (1963)	**104**
ZAPRUDER FILM: THE ASSASSINATION OF JOHN F. KENNEDY (1963)	79
ZATOICHI SESSHO TABI (1964)	117
ZOMBIE (1964)	57

ORGY PLUS MASSACRE
SEXY, SCARY & SENSATIONAL CINEMA 1950-1979

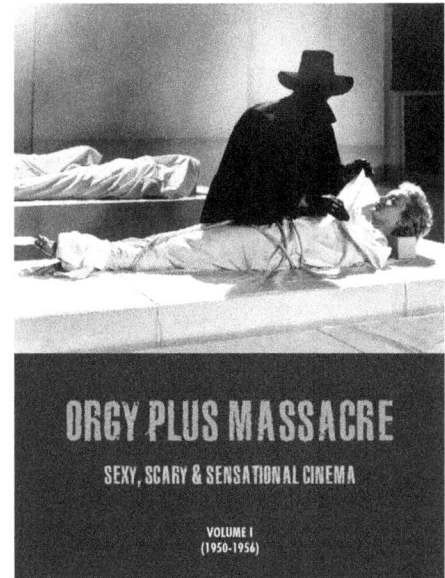

ORGY PLUS MASSACRE
SEXY, SCARY & SENSATIONAL CINEMA
VOLUME 1
(1950-1956)

ORGY PLUS MASSACRE
SEXY, SCARY & SENSATIONAL CINEMA
VOLUME 2
(1957-1959)

ORGY PLUS MASSACRE
SEXY, SCARY & SENSATIONAL CINEMA
VOLUME 3
(1960-1962)

ORGY PLUS MASSACRE
SEXY, SCARY & SENSATIONAL CINEMA
VOLUME 4
(1963-1964)

ORGY PLUS MASSACRE
SEXY, SCARY & SENSATIONAL CINEMA
VOLUME 5
(1965-1966)

SHADOWS IN A PHANTOM EYE

ATTRACTIONS & ABERRATIONS IN THE MOVING IMAGE 1872-1949

THE COMPLETE 15-VOLUME SERIES

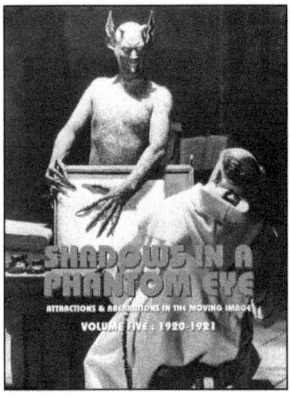   

www.ingramcontent.com/pod-product-compliance
Lightning Source LLC
Chambersburg PA
CBHW061125070526
44584CB00033B/4221